The Trouble with
Women in Power

DOMINIQUE GAULME

The Trouble with
Women in Power

Leaders Who Dared to Change the World

Flammarion

Pages 4–5:
Joan of Arc in battle.
Frank Craig, *The Maid*, 1907.

CONTENTS

FOREWORD

"A woman meddling in politics is as outrageous as a hen crowing instead of a rooster." So said Confucius—and he isn't alone in his thinking. Texts throughout history are explicit in defining the role of women, spelling out their parameters and limitations. The Bible is a veritable manifesto of casual misogyny, including St. Paul's statement that "the head of every man is Christ, the head of woman is man, and the head of Christ is God" (1 Corinthians 11:3). For centuries, women have been reduced to mere vessels for procreation. St. Thomas Aquinas—inspired, no doubt, by Hippocrates—said "*Tota mulier in utero*" (woman is all womb), an attitude echoed by Napoleon Bonaparte and many others.

Historically, women have been tied to the domestic sphere, which has excluded them from the political one. Many civilizations and nations through the ages did not even allow for the possibility of a female ruler. Salic law—which favors the male line in succession—permitted women to rule only for temporary periods, as regents waiting for their sons to come of age. In a few exceptional cases, women *did* ascend to power, yet Hatshepsut of ancient Egypt, Razia of India, and Maria Theresa of Austria were addressed by the male titles of pharaoh, sultan, and king, respectively.

And while Salic law may not have been observed everywhere, the dearth of female rulers throughout the world and across centuries cannot escape notice. It has been rare—except, perhaps, among the Celts or in Polynesia—for a people to say, "What if we were to choose a woman to lead our tribe, our land, our country?" Systemic and structural sexism has meant that women in power are the exceptions, often born into unique situations, or forced to overcome extraordinary circumstances.

Among the remarkable exceptions, a striking example occurred in eighteenth-century Russia. For almost a century, the vast country was run by women, with the succession of five tsarinas in a row—a stark contrast to the (male) rulers of modern-day Russia. Eighteenth-century Europe provided other opportunities for women to wield power, sometimes indirectly if they had the ear of the monarch, such as Madame de Pompadour in France. The influential *salonnières*—the hostesses whose salons welcomed the most important thinkers and writers of the day—contributed to the spread of Enlightenment ideals of equality and the Rights of Man and—thanks to the revolutionary Olympe de Gouges—Woman. Without the vote, however, women's ideas and wishes could be sidelined, and it was because of the pioneering nineteenth-century suffragists and their more radical sisters, the suffragettes, that the fight for women's right to vote was eventually successful, achieved first in New Zealand in 1893.

Women of color have been doubly oppressed by gender and race, and yet they have risen to the challenge. In the United States, Black abolitionists displaying indomitable courage—such as Harriet Tubman and Sojourner Truth—and women in the civil rights movement like Rosa Parks and Angela Davis have made their mark on history.

Things are changing, and today there are more women in positions of power than at any other time in history. However, there's still a way to go: at the beginning of 2020, only fifteen out of 193 countries were headed by women. But these women are bringing with them a new style of government. New Zealand's Jacinda Ardern has impressed the world repeatedly by responding to crises in her country with compassion and tolerance. The young female leaders of the Nordic countries—the youngest in the world—are facing global climate and humanitarian challenges head on. *Forbes* magazine went so far as to claim that countries led by women were more successful in their response to the COVID-19 pandemic.

Do women really govern better than men? Or is it that they encounter so many obstacles on their way to the top that only the truly exceptional make it? It has been said that "whatever women do, they must do twice as well as men to be thought half as good." And while women have been repeatedly subjugated throughout history, making sacrifices in both body and mind, their role in leadership—both directly and behind the scenes—is undeniable.

L.P.

Africa and the Middle East

Zenobia, Queen of Palmyra
by Edmund Dulac, 1937.

Tales of figures from Africa and the Middle East exist as much in the Western imagination as they do in historical reality. It is not always easy to separate fact from fiction. There are as many legends as there are certainties about Zenobia, who ruled in magnificent Palmyra, which rose from the sands of the Syrian Desert as though from some dream. And the story of Semiramis crying defiance to the invader from high up in the Hanging Gardens of Babylon has all the hallmarks of a beautiful fable.

What about Dido, who came from the east and founded Carthage? Told that the borders of her new land "had to fit into an ox-hide," the beautiful and cunning queen had the skin cut into such narrow strips that it could enclose a sizable kingdom. There are several versions of the tale, but none ends well. In one, having rejected a marriage proposal from a local king, Hiarbas, she had an immense pyre built and plunged headlong into the flames. In the *Aeneid*, her passion burns instead for Aeneas, whose departure leads to her killing herself with the very sword he left behind. Cleopatra, queen of Egypt, chooses to die from an asp bite to avoid being taken prisoner by the future Emperor Augustus and dragged behind his chariot. She is not the only woman to refuse such humiliation: Sophonisba, Carthaginian princess and queen of Numidia, also preferred death to being paraded in triumph by Scipio the African. The mysterious Queen of Sheba's story has a happier ending. After her encounter with King Solomon, she returned to her kingdom pregnant with Menelik I, founder of the dynasty of Ethiopia.

Above, top:
Semiramis Building Babylon
by Edgar Degas, 1861.

Above, bottom:
Dido and Aeneas, fresco from Pompeii,
Naples, first century CE.

Contemporary history in Africa and the Middle East is less rich in queens, except south of the Sahara, where in traditional monarchies "queen mothers" number in the hundreds. They share power with kings, and in Ghana there is even a queen mothers' association.

Women politicians, in the modern sense, are also gaining ground. In South Africa, Helen Suzman, an icon of progressive whites and opposition MP during apartheid from 1953 to 1989, fought tirelessly against racial segregation legislation. In the rest of the continent, it was not until the 1970s that women ministers began to appear: Princess Elizabeth of Toro, the foreign minister under Idi Amin, who was dismissed very quickly; Alda do Espírito Santo, minister and leader of the National Assembly of São Tomé e Príncipe; Graça Machel, wife of Samora Machel, Mozambique's first president in 1975, who became minister of education and who, after Machel died, married Nelson Mandela. The fate of Agathe Uwilingiyimana, Rwanda's first woman prime minister, was tragic: she was killed together with her husband and ten Belgian soldiers protecting her residence at the beginning of the genocide on April 7, 1994. Since the 1990s, the number of women ministers and women MPs in the continent has surged: since 2008, Rwanda possesses the highest female representation in parliament, with fifty-four out of eighty women members, while Ethiopia has a woman president, Sahle-Work Zewde.

Above, top:
Helen Suzman, South African politician and a symbol of the struggle of progressive whites against apartheid, in 1978.

Above, center:
Graça Simbine Machel, Mozambican militant for human rights and the rights of the child, widow of the first president of Mozambique, and later wife of Nelson Mandela, in 1999.

Above, bottom:
Sahle-Work Zewde, president of the Federal Republic of Ethiopia, in 2019.

HATSHEPSUT

(c. 1495–1468 BCE)

He? She? Pharaoh? "Pharaohess"? It was the polyglot genius and the decipherer of hieroglyphics Jean-François Champollion who, noticing some linguistic oddities at the site of Deir el-Bahari, first discovered the existence of Hatshepsut—known variously as the "queen-king," the "Mistress of the Two Lands," and the "daughter of Ra." Later, another French Egyptologist, François Auguste Ferdinand Mariette, excavated a gallery depicting the fabulous expedition ordered by the sovereign to the Land of Punt, a mysterious ancient kingdom beyond the Cataracts of the Nile.

It is not known if Hatshepsut actually had command of military operations, but she certainly rode in the vanguard of the expedition, the first to enter this land known for its sycamores, ebony, and aromatic Boswellia trees. The fleet returned loaded with Boswellia plants, which provided olibanum (also known as frankincense), as well as gold, ivory, ostrich eggs and plumes, and never-before-seen animals, such as the panther and the giraffe. A scene worthy of Hollywood then took place, as Hatshepsut smeared her body with a concoction of olibanum gum and water that made her skin glow like gold.

Although the veracity of her reign is not disputed, just how she acceded to the throne remains unclear. How did a woman—even if she were a pharaoh's daughter—manage to seize power and hold onto it for some twenty years? She claimed to be the daughter of the supreme god Amun-Ra who appeared to her in a dream, calling her his "dear daughter, his favorite, king of Upper and Lower Egypt, Hatshepsut." She was careful, on her statues at least, to present herself flat-chested and dressed as a (male) pharaoh, with loincloth, false beard, and a headdress, either identical to that of Tutankhamun or the *pschent*, the double crown.

Upon her death, the reign of Thutmose III began and, with it, Hatshepsut was expunged from history: images of her were destroyed and her name erased.

Head of the female pharaoh Hatshepsut as Osiris, discovered in the temple at Deir el-Bahari, Thebes, Egypt.

QUEEN OF SHEBA

(10th century BCE)

Which version would you like? She is mentioned in Biblical, Koranic, and Hebraic accounts, each with its own anecdote. All concur, however, that the mysterious Queen of Sheba came from Ethiopia. It is her homeland's version that characterizes her as Queen Makeda, the founder of a dynasty that was to reign until Haile Selassie I's death in 1975.

The Old Testament describes how the queen heard of Solomon's wisdom, and so rode into Jerusalem at the head of a caravan of camels carrying spices, gold, and precious stones, which she presented to the king. After this exchange of gifts, she returned home. In the Hebrew tradition she is described as worshiping the Sun, because of which Solomon summoned her to Jerusalem in order to convert her. Preceding her arrival, she dispatched ships laden with gifts. According to this version, Solomon had heard that the legendary queen had the legs and hooves of a donkey, and he had glass tiles laid on the floor in order to reveal her secret. When she arrived, the queen believed the tiles to be water and lifted her dress, revealing her very human—and hairy—legs.

The courtship of Solomon and Sheba took the form of a series of trials designed to test the other's wisdom. In one, the queen challenged Solomon to separate the boys from the girls in a group of identically dressed children. The king had a large basket of treats delivered to the children and invited them to help themselves. The boys lifted their tunics and filled them up, while the girls helped themselves more discreetly.

Solomon swore that he would not touch the queen as long as she took nothing from his palace. To get the better of her, he served her an extremely spicy banquet. Makeda woke with a raging thirst and poured herself a drink, breaking the agreement. The great king Menelik I was conceived from their union.

James Tissot,
Solomon and the Queen of Sheba, 1904.

CLEOPATRA

(69–30 BCE)

Cleopatra remains one of history's most famous female figures, millennia after her death.

She appears in countless guises. In painting, the very greatest artists tried to capture her allure, including Michelangelo. The nineteenth century adored depictions of her death—a perfect excuse for naked flesh and the "exoticism" that was fashionable at the time. Georges Méliès first put her on film in 1899, while Liz Taylor, in the 37-million-dollar version from 1963, created an indelible image of the beautiful, commanding queen. She has even been parodied, appearing in Uderzo and Goscinny's *Asterix and Cleopatra* and Alain Chabat's movie version of the same.

Cleopatra was actually a Greek queen, a descendant of Ptolemy, into whose lap Egypt had fallen with the division of Alexander the Great's empire. She was brought up in the Egyptian manner, that is to say, she was well educated: as well as reading and writing Greek, she studied arithmetic, epic poetry, tragedy, comedy, history, rhetoric, and numerous foreign languages.

Several legendary scenes from her life have been passed down through the ages, like a well-loved fable:

Scene 1: Aged sixteen, she emerges naked from a rolled-up carpet presented to fifty-year-old Julius Caesar. Subsequently, she seduces Caesar's lieutenant, Antony, with whom she dreams of building and ruling over an empire centered on the East. By then she wields power over the richest half of the ancient world.

Scene 2: The queen, at a banquet, removes her pearl earring, dissolves it in vinegar, and drinks the concoction. Pliny recounts the episode to the Romans as a morality tale, intending them to be disgusted by the decadence and luxury. It backfires. High-born Roman ladies are so fascinated by the tale that it launches a fashion for pearl vinegar.

Meanwhile, the future Augustus, incensed by Antony's purple and gold robes, loose living, and decadent Eastern tastes, advances upon Cleopatra's empire. In retaliation, she launches a fleet, but it is crushed at Actium.

This heralds the end of her dreams of a vast Eastern empire and the beginning of a final period of debauchery. Searching for an effective poison to end her life, she has various potions tested on prisoners awaiting execution.

Final scene: The queen takes her own life, offering her breast to the asp's bite. She is thirty-nine.

Curtain.

Facing page:
John William Waterhouse,
Cleopatra, c. 1887.

Pages 20–21:
Frederick Arthur Bridgman,
Cleopatra on the Terraces of Philae,
1896.

AMANISHAKHETO

(r. 35–20 BCE)

Far up the course of the Nile, lost among the burning dunes of the Nubian Desert, lay the kingdom of Kush: a dazzling, mysterious civilization little known today. After Augustus had vanquished Cleopatra, he was obliged to turn back and negotiate with Amanishakheto, or her mother Amanirenas, two powerful Black female pharaohs renowned for having held Roman forces in check between 25 and 21 BCE. Known as *kandakes*, the mothers or sisters of the king of Meroë ruled in their own right.

After preserving its independence for several centuries, this African kingdom then gradually sank beneath the sands of the Sudan. The reasons for its demise remain a mystery.

It was in 1822 that three French explorers unearthed more than two hundred small, steeply sloped pyramids: the necropolis of the queens of Meroë. In 1834, Giuseppe Ferlini—an unscrupulous Italian adventurer in the retinue of the viceroy of Egypt, Mehemet-Ali—raided what was probably the tomb of Amanishakheto, using explosives to dig out a fabulous treasure: bracelets, pendants, necklaces, neckpieces, and amulets made of gold and set with lapis lazuli, enamel, and glass paste.

In the kingdom of Kush, a heady mix of Egyptian, Hellenistic, and African influences had made for a unique style, which included the ram-headed effigies of Amun, the *ankh* cross, the *wadjet* eye, the *uraeus* cobra, and the *pschent* crown. Interestingly, on bas-reliefs of the *kandakes* and their court, the juvenile silhouettes of Egyptian women are replaced by full-bodied females with heavy breasts, rounded buttocks, and fleshy necks with "Venus rings" indicating physical maturity. Such uniqueness made it difficult for Ferlini to convince collectors that his hoard was authentic. Finally purchased by King Ludwig I of Bavaria, the collection now appears in museums in Munich and Berlin.

Facing page:
Stele representing the goddess Amesemi
with Queen Amanishakheto of Naga,
first century CE.

Above:
Gold bracelet with a winged goddess
wearing the double crown of Egypt,
first century CE.

ZENOBIA

(c. 240–274 CE)

By the third century CE, the once all-conquering Roman Empire was mired in a power struggle. Emperors followed one another in quick succession and the subjugated populations began to entertain dreams of freedom. The Persians even managed to capture Emperor Valerian, much to the Romans' disgrace, and it was Odaenathus, a Romanized Arab and ruler of Palmyra, who had to fight them at Rome's behest. Following the murder of Odaenathus and his son Herodianus, Odeanathus's widow, Zenobia, took the throne.

Zenobia came from the Hellenistic elite and was well educated. Exploiting Rome's weakness, she soon conquered an empire that was to be inherited by her son Wahballāt (Vaballathus). Invading Arabia, Palestine, and Egypt—the Roman Empire's breadbasket—she pushed on as far as Asia Minor.

During her reign, the desert city of Palmyra, celebrated for its magnificent architecture, became a cultural hub that attracted artists and philosophers.

The triumphant Zenobia, a legendary queen determined to make Rome her own, also captured the imagination. Depicted in imperial garb, she wore a helmet and garments edged in purple and trimmed with gemstones. On horseback or in a chariot, she adored hunting and drank with her generals. Living in a splendor inherited from ancient Persia she went one step too far: she issued coinage struck with her and her son Wahballāt as *Imperator* and *Augusta*, thereby signaling her claim on Rome. At this juncture, Aurelian rose to power; energetic and a fine strategist, he was intent on taking back the empire. One by one, he recovered the lands overrun by Zenobia, finally capturing the queen.

In 274, her conqueror had her paraded in triumph, led on a leash by a Persian jester. With gold shackles on her feet and hands, she was adorned with jewels so huge that she staggered under their weight.

Herbert Gustave Schmalz,
*Queen Zenobia's Last Look
upon Palmyra*, 1888.

KAHINA

(early 600s–703)

"After all, she was just a woman." So said Abd al-Malik, the Umayyad caliph of Damascus, as he opened the bag containing the head of Dihya, better known as Kahina.

Leader of the Jrawa tribe, in 688 she succeeded the great chief Kusaila and pursued his struggle against the Muslim conquest of the Maghreb in the seventh century. About thirty years before she was born, the Berber tribes had already begun to unite to stem the tide of the then new religion of Islam.

This Amazon, whose nickname means either "prophetess" or "witch," was said to have possessed magical powers. Jewish writers liken the name "Kahina" to "Cohen," meaning "the priest." Kahina repelled the army the Umayyad dispatched under the command of Hassan ibn al-Nu'man. According to legend, the latter asked the name of the most powerful king in Ifriqiya (now Tunisia), only to be told it was a woman.

At the first battle on the Wadi Nini, the Berber cavalry massacred the Arab forces. Pursued as far as Gabès, the Umayyad army was driven from Ifriqiya. Prisoners were legion, but Kahina gave them their freedom—all except for Hassan's nephew, Khalid ibn Yazid, whom she may have adopted, or taken as her lover, only to be betrayed by him. Like much that has been told about her personal life, history is not clear.

She governed an independent Berber state stretching from the Awras (Aurès) Mountains to the oases of Ghadames between 695 and 700–703. All too aware of the power of her enemies, she practiced a scorched earth policy to deter invaders, thus alienating the sedentary tribes around the oases.

When Hassan returned at the head of an army of several thousand, he subdued Gabès, Nefzaoua, and Gafsa. The clash took place in Tabarka: Kahina's army was defeated and the fierce warrior woman with fiery hair was slain in the amphitheater at El Djem.

Here, once again, various versions of her story exist: some say the Berber Boudicca (see p. 45) died sword in hand, others that she died by suicide, and others still that she was beheaded.

Marie Caire, known as Madame Jean Tonoir, *Head of a Woman from Biskra*, nineteenth century.

There are few depictions, if any, of Kahina, but this portrait may resemble her.

NZINGA

(1583–1663)

In their search for Prester John, the mythical Christian king of the East, Portuguese navigators ventured down the hitherto uncharted coast of Africa, entering its estuaries and sailing up its rivers. Passing the Congo, they ventured into Angola, whose king sent his sister Nzinga on an embassy to their governor at Luanda in 1622.

Nzinga arrived, dripping in gemstones and wrapped in multicolored feathers, impressing witnesses with her majesty and intelligence. During her stay she was baptized, taking the name Doña Ana de Sousa, with the governor and his wife acting as godparents.

Upon her return home, she discovered her brother had died. Inheriting the throne of Matamba, she began by eliminating all her rivals within the royal family. She then embarked on the ferocious resistance against the Portuguese that made her a national heroine, which she remains today.

For more than twenty years, Nzinga reigned with the support of bloodthirsty troops known as the Jagas. Father Cavazzi, who had gone on a mission to bring the Gospel to the country, referred to them in his writings and series of watercolors. He described her as a little woman, not beautiful but sharply intelligent. She was known to have taken countless lovers, and she held on to power through bloodshed and torture. Most striking was that Nzinga remained, above all, a warrior. At the head of her troops in battle, she was flanked by a guard of Amazons who fired arrows and hurled javelins.

At that time, Nzinga preferred to live naked, with her body painted and arms scarified, and sporting fierce-looking iron bracelets, but Cavazzi also portrayed her wearing layers of magnificent petticoats, made probably of "Kasai velvet," a textile from the Congo woven from palm fiber. Toward the end of her life, she reverted to her Christian faith, passing away at the age of eighty-one.

Beneath her queenly finery, gold brocade, and sumptuous jewels, she chose to be buried in the habit of a Capuchin.

Achille Devéria,
Portrait of Queen Nzinga Mbande,
c. 1830.

QUEENS
OF MADAGASCAR

An unexpected interlude in Madagascan history occurred in the nineteenth century: following the rule of the great King Andrianampoinimerina, four women succeeded one another on the throne, ensuring the political unity of the island.

The first, Ranavalona I (1788–1861), succeeded her husband in the wake of a military coup sparked by the arrival of English missionaries, whom she expelled. In 1835, she formally prohibited her subjects from adopting Christianity; the recalcitrant were arrested and some were executed. She also resisted the Westernization of the country and established a unique system in which the reigning queen always married the prime minister. Due to her fierce hostility to Europeans, they consistently described her as tyrannical and cruel. Nevertheless, to industrialize the country and erect the first royal palace to be built in stone, it was to two Frenchmen—Napoléon de Lastelle and Jean Laborde—that she turned.

On her death, she was succeeded by her son Radama II, but his reign was cut short when he was assassinated. His wife Rasoherina (1814–1868) inherited the throne, though real power lay in the hands of the prime minister. After a brief reign of five years, it was the turn of Ranavalona II (1829–1883). Unlike Ranavalona I, she reestablished links with English missionaries and opened the country up to the West.

The first ruler to be crowned Christian queen of Madagascar, in 1869 she declared Christianity the state religion, destroying the "*sampy*" (royal idols) and replacing them with the Bible. She also made education compulsory for children—both boys and girls—up to the age of fourteen. Other reforming measures included encouraging the construction of permanent buildings and forbidding slash-and-burn agriculture, in order to reduce the risk of fire.

She was succeeded by Ranavalona III (1861–1917), the last sovereign of Madagascar, who was overthrown by the French in 1897, following a military campaign to conquer the kingdom under General Gallieni. Exiled first to the island of Réunion, the queen ended her days in Algiers.

Facing page:
Philippe Ramanankirahina, *Portrait of Queen Ranavalona I*, early twentieth century. Andafiavaratra Palace coll., Ministry of Communication and Culture in Madagascar.

Above:
Queen Ranavalona III with the royal scepter, c. 1895.

ZAWDITU

(1876–1930)

The empress left the palace on the back of a mule adorned with gold, with her ladies in waiting, her confessor, and high dignitaries of the crown. She was dressed in a voluminous silk robe—red, maybe pink—with a black velvet mantle embroidered with birds and lions in gold thread. The last empress of Ethiopia, Zawditu symbolized the end of an empire that had its roots in the mythical union of King Solomon and the Queen of Sheba (see p. 17).

Ethiopia's history is steeped in blood and tears. A Christian enclave in the Muslim Horn of Africa, it was ravaged in the sixteenth century by the horsemen of Ahmed Gragn, known as "Ahmed the Left-handed," a Somali warrior only finally expelled by the Portuguese. In the nineteenth century, under Menelik, Ethiopia once again rode to victory, the only African country to overcome a European colonial power: Italy, in 1898.

Zawditu was the daughter of this great monarch and, following her father's death, kept vigil over his remains for several years. Power was then held by the emperor's grandson, Lij Iyasu, who had converted to Islam. Overthrown in 1917—thanks to help from the British, who suspected him of German and Turkish sympathies—he was replaced by Zawditu. An aristocrat, she delighted the great feudal lords, whereas the regent, Tafari Makonnen (the future Haile Selassie), was determined to modernize Ethiopia. Between them, they held sway over the empire, a mosaic of many peoples: Christians, Muslims, and animists.

Zawditu died in 1930, two days after her husband. The cause of death prompted many theories. Was it a broken heart? Had she succumbed to typhoid? Was it caused by her being plunged into a vat of cold holy water to chase out the fever? Was she poisoned by Tafari?

Ethiopia elected a female president, Sahle-Work Zewde, on October 25, 2018; she is the first woman to hold the post and currently the only female head of state on the African continent. Her power is broadly equivalent to Zawditu's, since the country is governed by the prime minister.

Empress Zawditu of Ethiopia
on the day of her coronation in 1917.
At her side, the Crown Prince,
Ras Tafari Makonnen (the future
Haile Selassie I).

GOLDA MEIR

(1898–1978)

In the early years of the twentieth century, in Milwaukee, Golda's little sister Tzipke caught sight of some mounted policemen in the local Labor Day parade. "Cossacks!" she yelled and fainted away. Golda, on the other hand, loved the air of festivity and the all-American aroma of popcorn and hotdogs. After Russia, the United States must have seemed strange to the girls, but Golda Mabovitch, the little Jewish girl from Kiev, was soon as Americanized as her older sister Sheyna was politicized. When her parents threatened to marry her off, curtailing her studies, Golda fled to Denver to live with her sister. It was at political meetings at Sheyna's home that Golda heard talk of a Jewish homeland, and she was soon dreaming of life on a kibbutz. It was also where she met Morris Meyerson, whom she agreed to marry—as long as he went with her to Palestine.

Inclined to action more than theory, Golda was convinced of her mission to work on a kibbutz, and at the age of twenty-three she left the United States. Upon arrival in the Middle East, she was immediately struck by the heat, dust, and clouds of flies; undeterred, she remained committed to life as a kibbutznik. Standing out for her militancy and zeal, she began her rise in the Histadrut, the future Labor Party. "Jewish observer from Palestine" at the Evian agreements in 1938, she was soon climbing the political ladder.

In 1948, she was one of the twenty-four signatories of the Declaration of Independence of the State of Israel. She became an ambassador, then labor minister, and foreign minister, with David Ben-Gurion calling her "the only man in his cabinet."

By February 1969 she was prime minister: Israel was twenty years old, while she was seventy-one. The intransigent "Iron Lady" denied the existence of a Palestinian people, which she thought of as an invention dreamed up to challenge Israel's sovereignty. The surprise attack by Arab nations on October 6, 1973, which sparked the Yom Kippur War, led to her resignation, despite the final victory.

She is known as the "grandmother of Israel," and female Israeli soldiers literally walk in her shoes—their military uniform includes orthopedic shoes dubbed "Goldas."

Golda Meyerson, known as Golda Meir, in May 1950.

ELLEN JOHNSON SIRLEAF

(born 1938)

An economist who studied in the United States, Ellen Johnson Sirleaf was the first woman elected by universal suffrage to head an African state, as president of Liberia from 2006 to 2018. During that time she received the Nobel Peace Prize, in 2011.

Liberia is an atypical country, which the American Colonization Society founded in 1822 to settle freed Black slaves, without deigning to consult the indigenous population. An American-style republic was established, led by the "Kongos," descendants of African Americans. In 1980, a coup d'état occurred during which local Staff Sergeant Samuel Doe executed the president and took his place. This marked the onset of a reign of terror that resulted in civil war. In 1997, the chief rebel leader Charles Taylor was elected president; he continued the conflict, exporting it to Sierra Leone, while still trafficking in arms and diamonds. Taylor was sentenced to fifty years in prison by a tribunal in The Hague for his part in the hundreds of thousands of deaths, rapes, and amputations that took place in Sierra Leone during that period.

At the time of the coup d'état, in 1980, Ellen Johnson Sirleaf was the finance minister, and it was her gender that saved her life. She fled to the United States where she worked for the World Bank and headed the African section of the United Nations Development Programme.

In 2006, when she was elected to succeed Charles Taylor as president of Liberia, her main task was to stabilize the country

with the help of UN forces. Putting a halt to arms trafficking, she lifted the sanctions with which the country had been burdened since her predecessor, and she re-engaged with the United States. Overcoming numerous difficulties, she strove to put her tormented homeland back on track. With little water or electricity, she endeavored to stem the Ebola epidemic of 2013.

Despite being somewhat controversial—she is suspected of tax evasion and defends laws criminalizing homosexuality, such as have been passed in many African countries—Ellen Johnson Sirleaf has succeeded in improving the image of her country and is a symbol of its return to peace.

Above:
Political activist Ellen Johnson Sirleaf in Monrovia, in 1986.

Facing page:
Ellen Johnson Sirleaf speaking at a White House summit on international development in the Ronald Reagan Building, Washington, D.C., in 2008.

Europe
and Russia

Europe has had no shortage of remarkable women, despite a history of institutional, legal, and social structures devised to curtail their opportunities. Individuals have been able to rise above these limitations, or even use them to their advantage. They may not all have had the personality of Spanish duchess Ana de Mendoza, Princess of Eboli—known as the "one-eyed Princess"—who so intrigued the court of Philip II, but there are many who have made their mark on history.

Take France, for instance. In the birthplace of feminism, women politicians today are still mocked, insulted, and whistled at in the National Assembly. Édith Cresson, the first and, as yet, only female head of government in France, kept her job for all of eleven months. But France has also given to the world the talents of one of the most powerful women: the always impeccably spoken and incomparably chic Christine Lagarde, who headed the IMF.

Spirited, intelligent women have always been a part of France's history, despite attempts by male intellectuals to denigrate and dismiss them. The women intellectuals known as "Précieuses" and lampooned in Molière's play were not remotely "ridiculous," they were simply loath to marry the geriatric boors society imposed on them. Long before Virginia Woolf, they just wanted "a room of their own," in order to write, like Madame de Lafayette and Madame de Sévigné. But Louis XIV put an end to their bid for independence and returned them to the protective arms of their fathers, husbands, and brothers. Nevertheless, their spirits continued to shine in salons presided over by exceptional women such as Madame Du Châtelet, Madame de Pompadour, Olympe de Gouges, and Madame de Staël—until the Revolution, and then Napoleon once again extinguished the flame.

Above, top:
Ana de Mendoza de la Cerda
by Sofonisba Anguissola, c. 1560.

Above, center:
Portrait of Anna Leopoldovna
by Ivan Yakovlevich Vishnyakov, c. 1740–46.

Above, bottom:
Portrait of Marie de Rabutin-Chantal,
Marquise de Sévigné by Claude Lefebvre, c. 1665.

England, unlike France, does not recognize the Salic law that prohibits women from acceding to the throne. It is a situation that benefited Elizabeth I, who was prepared to deprive her subjects of their heads if they crossed her. Everything changed with the arrival of the Hanover Dynasty in the eighteenth century and the creation of the post of prime minister backed by a parliamentary majority. This remains the state of affairs today, and it explains why sovereigns from Queen Victoria to Elizabeth II have reigned but not governed. Margaret Thatcher and Theresa May wielded more power than the queen, whose power is more or less confined to bestowing medals and titles.

Russia, where women seem to have taken a back seat, had a golden age for feminism in the eighteenth century, with five consecutive tsarinas, though not all were equally successful: Catherine I, widow of Peter the Great, who expired after two years of rampant excess; Anna Ivanovna, who carried a gun wherever she went and shot anything that moved; Anna Leopoldovna, regent for a year; Elizabeth I, Peter's whimsical, food-loving, sensual daughter, who had the end of *Hamlet* altered because it made her cry; and, finally, Catherine II—Catherine the Great—the philosophers' friend, who became an autocrat feared by everyone, including her own son Paul, who later forbade women from acceding to the Crown.

Today, gender equality is embodied by the Nordic countries, where female heads of government, ministers, and party leaders are legion.

Above, top:
Elizabeth II (Elizabeth Alexandra Mary Windsor), undated.

Above, center:
Theresa May when prime minister, December 2016.

Above, bottom:
Christine Lagarde at the launch of the COP26 private funding program in London in 2020.

LIVIA

(58 BCE–29 CE)

Busts of Livia—which typically depict her with a serious expression and an ornate hairstyle—give little inkling of the ruthless plans she is alleged to have hatched to get her sons into power.

When she and Octavian, the future Augustus, met, Livia was in the full bloom of youth and he, according to legend, was stunned by her beauty. No matter that they were both already married to other people. Head-over-heels, he abducted her at a banquet. Once divorced by special permit, Octavian and Livia were free to marry each other, but their forty-year union remained childless.

Livia was determined that one of her sons from her previous marriage should succeed her husband, and it seemed as though events conspired in her favor. When Octavian's direct descendants—children of his only daughter, Julia—mysteriously expired, Livia urged him to adopt her eldest son, Tiberius. Did she lend chance a helping hand? No one knows, but she was undeniably ambitious. To keep her husband's favor, she had no hesitation in providing him with young virgins; similarly, in another age and place, Madame de Pompadour would procure pretty mistresses for Louis XV.

Ostensibly, Livia epitomized the virtues of the Roman matron: dutiful, submissive, and humble. Simply attired—high-born Roman women only started to wear fabrics other than wool much later—she spun wool and wove her husband's clothes herself. As wife of the uncontested master of Rome, however, she was the first empress whose image was to become current—as much as that of her husband. Augustus went as far as to mint coins in her likeness, erecting public statues and even a portico on the Esquiline Hill where the pair appeared as Mars and Venus. When the emperor died, she withheld the news to give Tiberius time to hurry back to Rome and assume the throne.

She received the title Augusta posthumously, and thereby achieved divine status.

Livia as Ceres, bearing a sheaf of wheat and a horn of plenty, first century CE.

BOUDICCA

(30–61 CE)

Not all of Europe welcomed the conquering Romans. The French have Vercingetorix and the British have Boudicca, or Boadicea, the national heroine of resistance to Rome. The land of the Britons had been under the Roman yoke since 43 CE, the year Claudius set up colonies there. Though Caesar had made incursions further north, the northern Celts with their painted bodies proved even more terrifying than the Gauls.

On the death of her husband, Prasutagus, in 60 CE, Boudicca became queen of the Iceni, a people of present-day Norfolk and Suffolk in England. Seizing this pretext, the Romans invaded her wealthy kingdom, ransacking the land and destroying everything in their path. When Boudicca resisted, they flogged her and raped her two daughters. This only served to galvanize the queen, who, in retaliation, recruited a 120,000-strong army from her own and neighboring tribes. In accordance with Briton tradition, the army accepted military command from a woman without question.

While the Roman governor Caius Suetonius Paulinus was busy putting down a revolt in Wales, Boudicca plundered and set fire to the colony of Camulodunum (Colchester), massacring the legion dispatched to relieve the town. Then, before attacking Verulanium (St. Albans), she burned down Londinium (London), the commercial capital of the whole island and already heavily populated, as archaeological finds have shown. Tacitus estimates that about 70,000 citizens of Rome and their allies were slaughtered.

Learning of this, the governor redirected his army—the site of Boudicca's defeat is contested—and, after the initial Briton victories, the Romans, now better organized and better equipped, prevailed over the rebels. Nearly 80,000 Britons were killed and Boudicca fled with her daughters. It is said she poisoned herself—and perhaps them, too. Boudicca's legend in Britain, however, had only just begun, and over the centuries she would be associated with its queens Elizabeth I (see p. 61) and Victoria (see p. 82) as a symbol of the nation's strength.

Archibald Stevenson Forrest,
Queen Boudicca in the Forest, 1905.

THEODORA

(c. 500–548 CE)

If Rome lived for the Games in the Coliseum, then the heart of Byzantium beat for horse racing in the Hippodrome near the Imperial Palace. Emerging from the motley crew that gathered there was a young prostitute and actress, Theodora, daughter of a bear trainer. Spirited and bright, she bewitched Justinian, an intellectual who worked day and night, drank only water, dined abstemiously on pickled vegetables—and was the future emperor. Their vastly different social classes were initially an impediment: there was a law preventing governors from marrying actresses, which was amended in 524 to allow their marriage.

In 527, they were jointly anointed emperor and empress in the Basilica of Hagia Sophia, and Theodora soon became Justinian's most trusted adviser. During the Nika riots that rocked Byzantium, her composure and refusal to yield to the howling mob would save the emperor, who daydreamed of Augustan imperialism. As the rioters proclaimed a new emperor, Hypatius, she stood her ground and addressed the privy council, mustering their support and courage with the sublime phrase, "As for me, I agree with the ancient saying that royal purple is the noblest shroud." They would eventually triumph—an impressive performance for the daughter of an animal handler.

Perhaps remembering her own origins, she was involved in helping underprivileged women, particularly young, repentant prostitutes. She enacted many laws favorable to women, in a bid to give women the same legal rights as men. Under Justinian, it became legal for women to inherit and own property, as well as to buy and sell it and to borrow money. She outlawed brothels and pimping, made rape a capital offence, and set up a convent for former prostitutes who had repented.

On Theodora's death in 548, probably from breast cancer, Justinian was inconsolable. Despite surviving her by seventeen years, he only appeared in public again at the occasional official ceremony.

The magnificent mosaics at Ravenna, completed a year before her death, depict her in the company of Justinian: two parallel and symmetrical portraits symbolizing the equal rank and power of emperor and empress.

Byzantine school,
Empress Theodora with Her Court of Two Ministers and Seven Women,
detail of a mosaic in the Basilica of San Vitale, Ravenna, c. 547 CE.

CASTI
TATIS. EC
CLESIASTI
CÆQ LIBER
TATIS
AMICA

STIRPE. OPIBVS. FORMA. GESTIS.
ET NOMINE. QVONDAM
INCLYTA. MATILDIS. HIC IACET
ASTRA. TENENS

MATILDA OF TUSCANY

(c. 1045–1115)

Matilda's early years were eventful. When she was six, her father, Boniface III, Margrave of Tuscany, was assassinated with a poisoned spear. Her mother, Beatrice of Bar, remarried in order to secure her daughter's future. Her new husband had taken part in a rebellion against Emperor Henry III the Black, who, in retaliation, arrested Beatrice and Matilda. They were only released on the emperor's death, by which time Matilda was ten. She was also now sole heiress of the castle of Canossa, the marquisate of Tuscany, part of Lombardy, including Modena, Reggio, Mantua, Ferrara, and Cremona, and the earldom of Briey in Lorraine.

As well as studying Latin, French, and German, she was trained in the arts of warfare, which included not only horse riding, but also how to handle a spear, pike, axe, and sword. She also learned tactics and strategy, and how to lead an army, conduct a siege, and seize a stronghold. In the course of her debut military campaign in 1067, she expelled the Normans from Lazio.

In those days, Europe was dominated by two rival powers: the Holy Roman Empire, comprising Charlemagne's successors, and the Catholic Church. Elected in 1073, Pope Gregory VII was determined to improve the morality of the clergy. He also wanted to put a stop to the custom of princes appointing archbishops and bishops as a way of providing friends and family with land and income. This sparked what became known as the Investiture Controversy, during which Matilda took the side of the pope, who excommunicated the Holy Roman Emperor, Henry IV. Matilda offered to set up a meeting between Henry and the pope in her castle in Canossa, where the pontiff had taken refuge. After a perilous crossing of the snow-covered Alps, Henry arrived at the castle walls, where he was kept waiting for three days in a haircloth tunic before being able to make amends, thus confirming the enduring superiority of the Church over the Empire.

This famous episode was only the first act in a war during which Matilda showed her military talents to great effect. She died at the age of sixty-nine, but the conflict simmered on throughout the thirteenth and fourteenth centuries, becoming known as the conflict between the Guelphs (supporters of the pope) and the Ghibellines (supporters of the emperor). During her lifetime she was said to have founded one hundred churches, but evidence shows it to be many more. They made up important pilgrim routes during the Renaissance, and most of them are still in use today.

Paolo Farinati,
Allegorical Portrait of Matilda of Canossa, Countess of Tuscany,
c. 1587.

ELEANOR OF AQUITAINE

(1122–1204)

Whole volumes have been written about the life of Eleanor of Aquitaine. Heiress to Aquitaine and to Poitou, Eleanor wedded Louis VII, king of France, at the age of thirteen, giving him two daughters. The king was head over heels in love with his attractive queen, even if she shocked the Paris court with her exuberance, her southern charm, her plunging necklines, and her no-nonsense manner with men. Accompanying her husband on the Second Crusade, she grew tired of a king "more monk than husband" and sued for divorce. Their union dragged on for another three years: ample time for a dark legend to form around Eleanor. Too beautiful, too worldly, she was accused of having an affair with an uncle, as well as with Sultan Saladin, then aged eleven. Since there were no male descendants, the marriage could be annulled. Returning to her wealthy duchy, she married Henry Plantagenet, the future Henry II of England. Their union was fruitful: three girls and five boys.

Queen once again by marriage, she ruled jointly with Henry over a realm reaching from Scotland to Spain. Whenever her husband was away at war, Eleanor would ensure the regency. Nevertheless, the king's almost official liaison with his mistress, Rosamund Clifford, obliged her to regain her lands in Aquitaine, which she ruled from Poitiers.

It was their sons who stirred up trouble. Demanding a share of power, they gained the backing of their mother. Henry summoned Eleanor to England but she refused to go, seeking refuge in France disguised as a man and creating further scandal. This refuge was short-lived: she was captured by Henry's men and imprisoned for sixteen years.

On Henry's death in 1189, Richard—the famous Lionheart and Eleanor's favorite son—inherited the throne and immediately set his mother free. As soon as he was crowned, he returned to Poitou to entrust her with the regency of the kingdom. The last fourteen years of her life were spent arbitrating the conflict between Richard and his brother John "Lackland," and building the foundations of modern maritime law, before she retired to Fontevraud Abbey, Anjou, where she is buried.

Frederick Augustus Sandys,
Queen Eleanor, 1858.

JOAN OF ARC

(1412–1431)

Joan's power was won on the battle-field—even if she preferred waving a standard to wielding a sword. Her story seems like something from a fairy tale, featuring a young, uneducated shepherdess going to offer aid to the dauphin, who had taken refuge in the province of Berry, while an eight-year-old English boy in Paris claimed the French throne.

Her story has become the stuff of legend. During the Hundred Years' War, she had visions telling her to travel to the court of Chinon to offer her help to the future Charles VII against the English. He is said to have hidden among his lords to test her, but she walked straight up to him without a moment's hesitation. How did she persuade him to let her lead an army to liberate Orléans, thereby ensuring his coronation in Reims? She had no military experience at all, a mere peasant girl with a strong country accent who came to the dauphin following instructions "from God." What could she have whispered in his ear to convince him to appoint her as his warlord?

Thus opens the glorious epic of the "Maid of Orléans," as she was called, who is today known all over the world. Her successes were dazzling: on May 8, 1429, she lifted the siege of Orléans. A few weeks later, on June 18, she defeated the English at Patay. Then, after Troyes and Châlons-sur-Marne had been subdued, Charles VII was crowned king in Reims, on July 17, just as she had promised.

However, these triumphs did not last forever. After she failed to take Paris, the king and his counselors lost confidence in her. Seized by the Burgundians in Compiègne, she was handed over to the English. Her meteoric rise had lasted only a year and ended in martyrdom. After a year's imprisonment, on May 30, 1431, at the age of just nineteen, she was burned at the stake in Rouen. On the pyre was a paper miter inscribed with her crimes: heresy, relapsing, apostasy, and idolatry.

It should be noted that her execution had less to do with English policy than with her dressing as a man—which she did both on the battlefield and in prison. Wearing male clothing was a capital crime for a woman, condemned by the Bible and Christian tradition.

When the war ended, she was given a retrial at the request of her family, thirty years after her execution. In summing up, she was found innocent and declared a martyr. She has since become a cultural icon, a symbol of the Catholic Church and of France, and was made a saint in 1920.

Jean-Jacques Scherrer,
The Entry of Joan of Arc into Orléans,
1887.

ISABELLA I OF CASTILE

(1451–1504)

Despite her intelligence, culture, and spirit, Isabella was not destined to become the iconic queen of Spain. Engaged at the age of three to Ferdinand, heir to Aragon, she was sidelined from the court by her half-brother, Henry, successor to the Crown of Castile. She made the best of the situation by perfecting her education: from horse riding to the study of Aristotle, and from needlework to religion.

In 1469, she married Ferdinand, becoming queen of Castile on the death of Henry in 1474. The two spouses reigned in tandem, although each retained full powers over their respective realm.

The royal couple formed a united front and had big plans—first and foremost the completion of the Reconquista. To drive out the Muslims, Isabella herself led her troops against Granada, expelling King Boabdil from Spain after a six-month siege. For this reason, Pope Alexander VI would grant the couple the title of "Catholic Monarchs."

Spurred on by this success, Isabella pursued her conquests from the southern Mediterranean to the Canary Islands, recovering the kingdom of Naples from the French. However, Ferdinand and Isabella would then take a step too far in their determination to impose Catholicism on their territories. Goaded on by Tomás de Torquemada, they established the Inquisition, which hunted down Jews, Muslims, and even converts suspected of hypocrisy. To this day, this legacy continues to stall the process of Isabella's beatification.

Isabella's other great project came from her meeting with Christopher Columbus in 1492. She alone had faith in him and agreed to finance his expedition to the Indies via the west. In October of that year, he and his crew set foot in the Bahamas, which he immediately claimed for the Crown of Castile. Isabella's foresight and commitment ushered in the age of Spanish colonization. It was thanks to her that people later said the sun never set on the Spanish Empire.

Felipe Vigarny or Biguerny,
Entry of the Most Catholic Kings and of Cardinal Cisneros into Granada,
relief on the main altarpiece in the royal chapel at Granada Cathedral,
sixteenth century.

Attributed to Michel Sittow,
court painter to the queen,
La Virgen de la Mosca, also known as
the *Altarpiece of Isabella the Catholic*,
1520.

CATHERINE DE' MEDICI

(1519–1589)

France may not have had a "queen regnant," but this does not mean it has never been ruled by a powerful female monarch.

In 1533, Catherine de' Medici arrived from Italy to wed the future Henry II, bringing with her such novelties as heeled shoes, the "*bride à fesses*" (an ancestor of the culotte), the fork, new varieties of pastries, and a woman's saddle. She was a skilled rider and dancer, and her father-in-law, Francis I, was clearly delighted with her.

This period in French history was racked by the religious strife that led to the Wars of Religion. After a reign of twelve years, Henry II was killed during a tournament and Catherine, then forty, went into mourning for the rest of her life. Her black clothing struck fear in onlookers: at this time, it was customary for the queens of France to wear white for mourning.

She was regent during the minority of her son Charles IX, and as queen mother was the real power behind the throne. She stopped at nothing to ensure peace—neither negotiations nor executions. She was ingenious, cunning even: she created a "flying squadron," a group of beautiful women who were dispatched to monitor and entrap potential enemies. Her reputation as a poisoner and plotter, however, was more fiction than fact.

Facing page:
François Clouet, *Catherine de' Medici*, c. 1556.

Pages 58–59:
French school, *Ball at the Court of Henry III on the Occasion of the Wedding of Anne, Duke of Joyeuse, to Marguerite de Vaudemont*, c. 1581.

Festivities were another of Catherine's weapons and she treated them as an arm of government—what is known today as "soft diplomacy." Traveling all over France with her children and courtiers, she organized hunts, dances, theatrical performances, concerts, and tournaments. Though she led the royal procession through Catholic and Protestant towns alike, negotiating tirelessly, her efforts were in vain and the religious wars continued.

The queen was also strategic when it came to marrying off her children, who made eminently political unions. Catholic daughter Marguerite wed the leader of the Huguenots, Henry of Navarre, in 1572, in a bid to end religious tensions. Mass was celebrated on August 18; from August 19–21, dances and pageants were held to celebrate the union; but on August 22, St. Bartholomew's Day, religious animosity erupted into the brutal massacre of Protestants, resulting in an estimated 3,000 deaths in Paris and 30,000 throughout the kingdom.

History remains undecided on Catherine de' Medici's role in the massacre. She appeared to want Catholics and Protestants to live together peacefully, but could she instead have deliberately unleashed such an outburst of violence in order to further her own interests? Or was she just an innocent bystander? Recent historians tend to minimize her active role, but the image of the plotting queen dressed all in black—even a fictional one—casts a long shadow.

ELIZABETH I

(1533–1603)

She had a difficult start in life: her father was the English Bluebeard, Henry VIII, and her mother was Anne Boleyn, a "seductress" who was beheaded at the king's command.

The long reign of Elizabeth (1558–1603) is marked, like her father's, by the doctrinal disputes that followed the Reformation. Raised as a Protestant, she converted to Catholicism to avoid the wrath of her fearsome sister, Mary I—"Bloody Mary." However, once Elizabeth had ascended the throne, she reverted to the Anglican faith devised by her father.

She was known as the Virgin Queen for her categorical refusal to wed. This led to a great deal of speculation and gossip: was it due to a physical problem that, in the words of Ben Jonson, "made her uncapable of man"? Or was her refusal motivated by a determination not to share power? She may have had many suitors—including Catherine de' Medici's youngest son, the Duke of Anjou, who was twenty-two years her junior—and enjoyed male company, but she governed alone.

It was thus on her own that she confronted the Spain of Philip II, sending out Francis Drake with the English fleet against Spanish galleons laden with gold. In 1588, the English fleet crushed Philip's Invincible Armada, a feat for which Drake was knighted. Four years earlier, another of her favorites, Walter Raleigh, explored the east coast of North America, naming it "Virginia" in her honor and going on to found a permanent colony.

A tireless horsewoman and, like her father, a keen hunter, she would gallop, hunting with falcon, often alone. She even had the manes and tails of her horses dyed the same color as her famous red hair.

Like many princesses of the time, Elizabeth was also highly cultured. Her reign is known as the "Golden Age"—the Elizabethan era of William Shakespeare, Christopher Marlowe, and Ben Jonson. There were talented painters, too, as attested by the quality of the many portraits of the queen; she disliked sitting for them, but had grasped the importance of portraiture as a propaganda tool.

Despite her successes and her aura, however, Elizabeth I's reign was tarnished by the iniquitous trial and execution of Mary Stuart, Queen of Scots, her rival and claimant to the English throne.

Nicholas Hilliard,
Queen Elizabeth I, c. 1592.

CHRISTINA OF SWEDEN

(1626–1689)

When she was born she was so hirsute and her voice so loud that the midwives mistakenly told her parents they had a boy. Her father, Gustav II Adolf, known as the Great, adored her; on hearing the mistake he said, "She'll be clever! She made fools of us all." Her mother, prone to melancholy, was less enthusiastic, complaining that the baby was ugly and dreaming of the infant's death.

Portraits of Christina of Sweden show a strong face, with dark hair and expressive eyes—nothing like the blonde, sublime Greta Garbo of the 1933 film. There is speculation that she may have been intersex: a contemporary described her as having the mouth of Venus and the gait of Mars. On the death of her father, she took the official title of "king" and attempts were made to find her a husband, but no one suited. Highly educated, she had a passion for philosophy, corresponding with Pascal, Leibniz, and Spinoza, and inviting Descartes to Sweden, where he died not long after. Questioning the traditional roles of men and women, and a devotee of military heroines, she wore men's dress and was horrified at the idea of childbirth. Yet she was in favor of Salic law and believed that women in power were ridiculous, finally abdicating in 1654 after a reign of twelve years.

Dressed as a man, she left her country on horseback, heading south. By the end of the year, she had converted to Catholicism. She struck awe in everyone she met: the "Pallas of the North" became the darling of the European courts and a friend of scholars and writers. In France, she met the two women she most admired: Ninon de Lenclos, the famous courtesan, and the Grande Mademoiselle, cousin of King Louis XIV. But the French court began to tire of her unconventional ways. The final straw came when she had her favorite, Monaldeschi, executed in the Château of Fontainebleau, and she was forced to leave.

In Italy, the royal convert was enthusiastically received by the pope and the nobility, who treated her to rounds of festivities. Her erudition and intellectual curiosity delighted, although her constant challenges to the established order eventually became wearing. The most famous and most capricious female sovereign of her time—who wanted neither children nor kingdom, and who had dazzled all Europe—remained in Rome for the rest of her life, under the pope's protection and control. After an elaborate funeral, she was buried in the papal crypt in St. Peter's Basilica.

Sébastien Bourdon,
*Equestrian Portrait of Christine,
Queen of Sweden*, 1652–54.

THE GRANDE MADEMOISELLE

(1627–1693)

One anecdote in particular encapsulates the extraordinary, fantastic fate and the strange character of Anne Marie Louise d'Orléans, Duchess of Montpensier, known as the "Grande Mademoiselle": aged eleven, she was told, jokingly, that she would marry her newborn cousin, the future Louis XIV. She firmly believed it to be true, until she was put straight by Cardinal Mazarin.

The Grande Mademoiselle—niece of King Louis XIII and daughter of Gaston d'Orléans, known as "Monsieur"—was born in the Palais du Louvre. When she was just five days old, her mother died, and, though she was close to her father, she would spend part of her life compensating for his involvement in conspiracies against the king and his advisor, Cardinal Richelieu.

What she lacked in beauty she made up for in wealth, courage, and determination. During the Fronde, the French civil war that broke out in 1648, she heroically stood by her father in his plots against his nephew, Louis XIV. She was physically daring: in her memoirs she described how she was smuggled into Orléans to rally the population in his favor, leaping over hedges and "climbing like a cat." Then, while in Paris, to save the Grand Condé, one of the leaders of the "Fronde des Princes," she cannoned the king's troops, leading to five years' exile in Burgundy.

In middle age, she confronted royal authority once again. The cause was an affair of the heart: she had fallen for Lauzun, a nobleman but notorious womanizer. The queen and court heartily disapproved of the union, so Louis XIV attempted to dampen the seducer's ardor by sending him off to the fortress of Pignerol, where he remained for ten years.

In an effort to obtain Lauzun's freedom, the Grande Mademoiselle agreed to give up a large part of her fortune to the Duke of Maine, Louis XIV's favorite illegitimate son, and make him her heir. Following Lauzun's liberation, a secret marriage was contracted, but the union between the adventurer and the elderly Mademoiselle was not a happy one. Their married life became a succession of arguments, reconciliations, and even violence. Finally, she had to drive him away.

Now no more than tolerated at court, primarily due to her chilly manner and notorious avarice, Anne Marie Louise d'Orléans turned to religion, living in the Palais du Luxembourg until her death from cancer in 1693.

Louis Ferdinand Elle (the Elder), *Portrait of Anne Marie Louise d'Orléans, known as La Grande Mademoiselle*, c. 1660.

MADAME DE MAINTENON

(1635–1719)

Madame de Maintenon—born Françoise d'Aubigné, into a good yet impoverished family—was an enigmatic figure who would become the second wife of the Sun King.

Though raised in the Catholic faith, her grandfather was the Huguenot poet Agrippa d'Aubigné. Spending six years in Martinique, she earned the nickname the "beautiful Indian." Upon her return to France, her family faced serious financial difficulties and Françoise never forgot the hunger, cold, and humiliation of those years.

To avoid being sent to a convent, at the age of sixteen she married Paul Scarron, a writer of burlesques who was twenty-five years her senior and paralyzed. She held salons that were legendary, frequented by the wits of the day, and a meeting place for the spirited women known as the "Précieuses." Madame de Montespan and the writers Madame de Lafayette and Madame de Sévigné were regular attendees, and they formed a network of attractive and intelligent women.

On Scarron's death, she was employed to supervise the illegitimate children the king had fathered with Madame de Montespan. On his visits, His Majesty was struck by her genuine affection for his offspring, and he grew to enjoy the company of "Widow Scarron," fueling the jealousy of Madame de Montespan. When Madame de Montespan became compromised in the "affair of the poisons"—a major scandal in which members of the aristocracy were accused of poisoning and witchcraft—the king dismissed her.

Around this time, both the queen and Mademoiselle de Fontanges—the sovereign's latest young mistress—died. The only woman left close to the king was Françoise, now Marquise de Maintenon, who had become his friend, his confidante, his mistress, and, finally, in a secret wedding ceremony, his wife.

Now married to the most awe-inspiring monarch in all Europe, she founded the Maison Royal de Saint-Louis, also called the Maison de Saint-Cyr, an institution dedicated to bringing up young girls who were in the position she had once been in: well-born, but impoverished. By then, her religious faith had begun to assert itself, and the Marquise de Maintenon urged Louis XIV to look to his salvation. Under her influence, he fought against Protestantism, and in 1685 he revoked the Edict of Nantes protecting the rights of Protestants. In the same vein, he reinforced persecution against the Jansenists and the Quietists.

Despite the challenges of attending to a cantankerous and egocentric king, the marquise continued her political and advisory role until the death of the sovereign in 1715. She followed him to the grave in 1719, but her legacy, particularly through her school and its promotion of educational equality, was felt throughout the century.

Pierre Mignard,
Portrait of Françoise d'Aubigné,
Marquise de Maintenon,
seventeenth century.

ELIZABETH OF RUSSIA

(1709–1761)

Daughter of the formidable Tsar Peter the Great and his second wife, an illiterate serving girl, Elizabeth had to wait for three other women to ascend her father's throne before she could wield power. First her mother, Tsarina Catherine I, who died after two years of carousing; then her cousin Anna Ivanovna, who reigned for ten years; and then Anna Leopoldovna, regent for the infant Ivan IV for a year.

It was during this regency that "Peter's daughter," as the army called Elizabeth, staged a coup d'état, on November 25, 1741. Flanked by the Preobrazhensky Guard, whose uniform she wore, she rode into the palace, seized power, and proclaimed herself empress.

She was charismatic and enjoyed luxury, draping herself with diamonds, precious fabrics, and rare furs. She was a great gourmet, and her reign was an endless round of balls, feasts, travels, and affairs with any man or woman who took her fancy.

As unpredictable as she was beautiful, she was fond of wearing men's clothes to show off her legs and ordered men to dress as women, laughing out loud at the sight of them in their panniers and restrictive clothing. Her court spoke French, introduced to the nobility by Peter the Great, and she attracted many artists to Russia.

On the diplomatic front, she entered the Seven Years' War alongside Austria and France, dispatching an 80,000-strong army to Prussia. In 1760, her troops marched into Berlin.

Her abiding passions, however, remained music and architecture. Her taste for the baroque enriched St. Petersburg with a new Winter Palace on the Neva River, the Anitchkov Palace on the Fontanka, the marvelous Smolny Convent, and Tsarkoye Selo, inspired by Versailles.

Over the years, the fresh-faced tsarina began to fill out and drink to excess. She dispensed corporal punishment liberally, slappping, beating, or whipping for the most minor of offences. Her rivals in beauty or fashion were sent to Siberia, or had their tongues cut out. Yet on taking power, she had sworn never to impose the death penalty—a promise she kept throughout her reign.

She was responsible for choosing the wife of the future Peter III, her nephew and heir to the throne. She selected a minor German princess, Sophie Friederika Augusta von Anhalt-Zerbst. This minor princess would become Catherine the Great (see p. 74).

Louis Caravaque,
Portrait of Grand Duchess Elizabeth Petrovna, 1720.

MARIA THERESA OF AUSTRIA

(1717–1780)

She galloped up the mountainside overlooking Pressburg (Bratislava) and, following tradition, brandished the sword of St. Stephen to the four cardinal points. Thus began the reign of the great Maria Theresa, "king" of Hungary (Hungary's constitution did not recognize the possibility of a queen), archduchess of Austria and queen of Bohemia, known as the "empress," since her husband Francis I and then her son Joseph were officially emperors in the Holy Roman Empire.

At the age of twenty-three, she engaged in the War of Austrian Succession against Prussia, Bavaria, Saxony, France, Piedmont-Sardinia, and Spain: a true female warrior. But she was also a wife, a lover, and mother to sixteen children—six of whom did not reach adulthood. Over the years, the pretty young woman would grow into a formidable matron.

It is hard to imagine how she juggled pregnancy, childbirth, and combating Frederick II of Prussia, all the while administering her states. While she strengthened the army, she also went about modernizing the Austrian Empire, which included education reform, making school compulsory for children from the ages of six to twelve.

Keeping her subjects under constant surveillance, Maria Theresa issued a raft of legislation. She instituted a "vice squad," the "chastity commissioners," to stamp out prostitution and keep unaccompanied women off the streets of Vienna. She divided Austrian society into three classes, who had to wear clothing and accessories in keeping with their rank.

Yet, despite these harsh policies, Maria Theresa loved festivities: when four months' pregnant, she danced at Schloss Möllersdorf on Shrove Tuesday, then returned to Vienna for a costume ball, followed by a masked ball, and finally attended Mass on Ash Wednesday.

However, the empress's everyday life was a simple, family one: breakfast in a robe and nightcap, while the children played on the floor. She negotiated marriages for many of her children with European royal and noble families, including her daughter Marie Antoinette, queen of France, to whom she wrote a steady stream of letters packed with advice. A century before Queen Victoria (see p. 82), Maria Theresa was indeed "the grandmother of Europe."

Martin van Meytens,
Maria Theresa Riding Up Coronation Hill,
mid-eighteenth century.

MADAME DE POMPADOUR

(1721–1764)

One day, when Louis XV was out hunting in the forest of Sénard, a blue phaeton carrying a beautiful young woman dressed in pink swept past. The next day, the phaeton was pink and the ravishing figure in blue. The king, entranced, made his move. These enticing sightings were not by chance—far from it. They had been stage-managed by the Pâris brothers, wealthy *fermiers-généraux* who collected tax on behalf of the king. Using their beautiful protégé, Jeanne Poisson, the future Marquise de Pompadour, as bait, they planned to obtain grace and favor from the king.

The court at Versailles judged this new favorite by her social origins—Parisian new money—and predicted no more than a brief fling with His Majesty. Yet their relationship was to endure nineteen years, with nothing and no one able to come between them. Louis XV, known as the *Bien-Aimé* (the Beloved), was radiantly happy, while Jeanne understood how to transmute what was a physical attraction into a powerful bond of trust, kindness, and friendship. She added a good dose of patience and listening, because the king was a depressive whose spirits only the beautiful marquise could raise. Wisely, she took care to win over the queen, Marie Leszczyńska.

Pretty, piquant, and cultured, she backed the publication of the *Encyclopedia*, the Enlightenment's magnum opus. She frequented writers and artists, sang at the opera, and was known for her exquisite style: Madame de Pompadour was surely the first true *Parisienne*. Her clothes were universally imitated: French-style gowns with Watteau pleats; light fabrics of all colors; smaller panniers. In private, she wore "sultana" outfits with wide pantaloons. She started the fashion for unpowdered hair, her head adorned instead with pearls or flowers.

Playing a role equivalent to prime minister, her political clout was considerable. Louis XV amazed all Europe by signing a treaty of alliance with Maria Theresa of Austria (see p. 70), thereby putting an end to the standoff with the Habsburgs. This turnaround was to the detriment of the Prussia of Frederick II, who loathed the three women who brought it about— the "League of the Three Petticoats" consisting of Maria Theresa of Austria, Tsarina Elizabeth of Russia (see p. 69), and Madame de Pompadour.

Maurice Quentin de La Tour,
*Portrait of the Marquise de Pompadour,
Jeanne Antoinette Poisson,*
1752–55.

73

CATHERINE THE GREAT OF RUSSIA

(1729–1796)

After hurtling through Russia in a sable-lined sled pulled by ten white horses, Sophie Friederika Augusta von Anhalt-Zerbst, the impoverished German princess chosen by Tsarina Elizabeth (see p. 69) to marry the heir to the throne, at last met the empress herself: tall, beautiful, and dripping in diamonds.

During this meeting, Sophie realized that it was in her best interests to become Russian. She quickly picked up the language and was baptized into the Orthodox faith, taking the name Catherine. Staggering beneath the weight of silver brocade and sumptuous jewels, Catherine wed Grand Duke Peter Ulrich. It was not a fairy-tale wedding and he was not a fairy-tale prince. His face was pockmarked and his sole distractions were alcohol, dolls, and putting his toy soldiers through military exercises. Catherine took refuge in reading and spent nine years devouring the works of Roman and French Enlightenment thinkers: Tacitus, Montesquieu, Voltaire, and Madame de Sévigné, to name but a few.

Still, the couple required an heir, so Elizabeth made her take a lover, and Paul, the future emperor, was born. The affair was the first of many. After Elizabeth's death, Peter ascended the throne and was soon universally detested. Barely six months into his reign, and urged on by officers of the Imperial Guard, Catherine rode into St. Petersburg wearing the uniform of the Preobrazhensky Guard and had her husband dethroned. The emperor was imprisoned and later assassinated.

After the indolent Elizabeth, here was an intellectual tsarina, who rose at five o'clock every morning to work. Composing the Nakaz, or Instruction, a study of political theory inspired by Montesquieu, she promoted vaccination, built a foundling hospital, established the Smolny Institute on the model of Madame de Maintenon's Maison de Saint-Cyr, and introduced her vast country to the potato. She reformed every domain—except the peasantry and serfdom. She placed a woman, Princess Dashkova, at the head of the Imperial Russian Academy. As a patron of the arts, she ushered the Enlightenment in to Russia, inviting artists, writers, and thinkers to her court. She employed a woman sculptor, Marie-Anne Collot from France, to sculpt many members of the court, including the head of Peter the Great for Étienne Maurice Falconet's equestrian monument.

Dreaming of conquering Constantinople, she realized the ambitions of Peter the Great and extended the empire toward the Volga and the Black Sea, to the detriment of the Turks. It was Catherine, known as an Enlightened despot, who turned Russia into a power of the first rank, and whose reign is considered the Golden Age of Russia.

Portrait of Catherine II in Traveling Dress, after the original of 1787 by Mikhail Shibanov.

OLYMPE DE GOUGES

(1748–1793)

Born during the reign of Louis XV, Marie Gouze—not yet Olympe de Gouges—was brought up in the Age of Enlightenment in a France where women were celebrated. Power resided partly in the pretty hands of Madame de Pompadour (see p. 73), and Paris hummed with the conversations in the salons of Madame du Deffand and Madame Geoffrin. The writers and thinkers who flocked to them talked about culture, of course, but also about free speech and equality.

Meanwhile, in distant Montauban, a beautiful young girl was married off to a man thirty years her senior, who drowned following the birth of their son. The twenty-year-old widow moved to Paris and adopted the name Olympe de Gouges. Rejecting the offer of marriage from a high-ranking civil servant in the Navy, she instead embarked on an affair with him that would last until the Revolution.

Polished, financially secure, and attractive, she frequented the city's salons and began to write. She set up her own theater company, becoming famous with the play *Zamore and Mirza*, a condemnation of slavery that triggered outrage and threats from plantation owners and ultra-royalists alike. But Olympe was not deterred and continued writing—reports, columns, brochures, and posters, which she had printed at her own expense. Describing a better world, her writings spurred the king into action. In the early days of the Revolution, Olympe's involvement was sporadic. An admirer of Mirabeau, she proposed mustering a female National Guard. As the Revolution gathered pace, so did Olympe's engagement. In 1792, she dedicated her celebrated *Declaration of the Rights of Woman and the Female Citizen* to the queen.

Pro-divorce, she campaigned for the suppression of the marriage sacrament and its replacement by a civil contract, as well as for the right to sue for paternity. She also called for the creation of maternity units so that women would not have to give birth in general hospitals, for state workshops for the unemployed, and for shelters for beggars.

A true feminist before the term was coined, she opposed Marat and Robespierre and ended her life on the guillotine, in the midst of the Terror, on November 3, 1793.

Anonymous,
*Portrait of Olympe de Gouges
(Madame Aubry)*, 1798–1801.

LOUISE OF PRUSSIA

(1776–1810)

The ravishing, lively Louise of Prussia—like a real-life fairy-tale princess—bewitched everyone she met. Goethe referred to her "celestial appearance," while Élisabeth Vigée Le Brun—Marie Antoinette's favorite painter—praised the beauty of her figure and the "dazzling freshness of her complexion." All rhapsodized about her kindness, charm, and majesty. (All, that is, except Napoleon, who remained as impervious as a "waxed cloth over which all that glides.") She was even compared to Joan of Arc and became the object of a veritable cult in Germany, where she was seen as the mother of the homeland.

Daughter of Charles II of Mecklenburg-Strelitz, the future Queen Louise preferred dancing to studying. In 1793, she married the heir to Prussia, the future Frederick William III. At first, Louise felt lonely, but then the couple moved to Paretz, where they created a German "Petit Trianon": rusticity, peasant revels, pregnancies. It all went swimmingly.

France, however, was growing restless. In 1804, the arrest and subsequent execution of the Duke of Enghien on false charges of conspiracy against Napoleon outraged European courts. Nevertheless, the king of Prussia refused to go to war. At the instigation of the warmongers, Queen Louise, Tsar Alexander I, and Frederick William III forged an alliance by the tomb of Frederick the Great, but Napoleon crushed the Austrians at Austerlitz in 1805 and, the following year, dissolved the Holy Roman Empire.

In the face of her husband the king's resistance to declare war, Louise urged him on, calling the new emperor of the French a "monster" and "scourge of the earth." The Prussian army was no longer what it had been under Frederick the Great, however, and was once again routed by Napoleon at Jena and at Auerstadt by Davout. "Napoleon blew on Prussia and Prussia ceased to exist," said the German poet Heinrich Heine. The royal family fled. Russia was defeated in 1807 at Friedland, and the two emperors met at Tilsit to negotiate. Louise, following a meeting instigated by Napoleon, came away empty-handed.

She died in 1810 without seeing the fall of her enemy, but she would be avenged by her son William I, who vanquished Napoleon III in 1870, during the Franco-Prussian war.

Josef Grassi,
Portrait of Queen Louise of Prussia,
1802.

ÉLISA BONAPARTE

(1777–1820)

In Napoleon's eyes, the ideal woman was his beautiful sister Pauline, who was no great intellect but an excellent dancer and hostess. His sister Caroline was the voluptuous one, while Élisa— the eldest, the least attractive, but the most intelligent—resembled her fearsome brother.

Raised the hard way at the Maison de Saint-Cyr—the institute for impoverished girls of the aristocracy—on the outbreak of Revolution Élisa returned to Ajaccio with an education that was to serve her and the emperor well. On the quiet, she wed a Corsican officer, Pasquale Baciocchi, known as Félix, who remained by her side throughout the imperial odyssey.

After Napoleon seized power, Élisa observed his wife Josephine's role as a leader of fashion, which set her to thinking. Élisa, now titled Princess of Piombino and Lucca, used her status to aid French industry, and she demanded that ladies of the court wear textiles from Lyon. When she became Grand Duchess of Tuscany, she undertook reforms and became interested in the arts and archeology. Establishing cotton plantations in Piombino, she developed the use of Carrara marble, drained marshes, built roads, and improved the lives of women. Modeled on the Institut Félix for boys, the Institut Élisa in Lucca represented the best female education at the time. Her plans for improvements were not always welcome, however: keen to leave her mark, like her brother, she had the Church of the Madonna dei Miracoli— a Renaissance masterpiece to which the people of Lucca were very attached— razed to the ground to make way for an esplanade and a colossal statue of the emperor.

In Florence, she sought to return to its former glories the Accademia della Crusca, an institution dedicated to purifying the Tuscan language that dated back to 1582. Nurturing the idea of founding an exclusively female academy in Paris, she even designed its uniform, but such projects remained on the drawing board.

All the while modernizing her states, Élisa enjoyed the social whirl, throwing party after party, right up to the Battle of Waterloo. She was the first of the Bonaparte siblings to die, in Trieste, in 1820.

Guillaume Guillon Lethière,
Maria-Anna known as
Élisa Bonaparte, Princess of Lucca
and of Piombino, Grand Duchess
of Tuscany, 1809–14.

QUEEN VICTORIA

(1819–1901)

Viewed by posterity as a stout old woman in black, Victoria stood at the head of the British Empire for sixty-three years and is one of Britain's longest-reigning monarchs. She is also associated with an almost laughable prudery, although the reality is quite the opposite. As a young princess, she fell for practically every man she met. As a married queen, she described her delight on her wedding night at the sight of Prince Albert's magnificent legs. She was less keen on the children who were the inevitable result of married life: there were nine in all, over seventeen years. She relished her time alone with her husband, on summer vacations without the children. At the death of Albert, aged only forty-two, she was inconsolable and would remain in mourning for the rest of her life.

During her long reign, Victoria restored the image and strengthened the role of the monarchy, earning her universal respect after the debauched behavior of her uncles who preceded her. She won over her people initially by her freshness and youth, and later by her moral rigor. She increased the bonds between monarch and subjects by engaging in civic duties and becoming patron of 150 institutions, from charities to culture, ensuring the visibility of the royal family.

"Victorianism" was instrumental in democratizing political life in Britain and in ushering the country into the industrial age. The vote was extended to the male working class, doubling the voting population. Technology and industry flourished under her reign, as showcased in the Great Exhibition of 1851.

Although her role as monarch demanded political neutrality—the monarchy had had its political powers drastically reduced—her influence was felt both at home and abroad. Thanks to Victoria's management of diplomatic relations between France and Britain, the two countries had never been so close. Initially won over by Louis-Philippe I and his family, she subsequently, and far less expectedly, hit it off with Napoleon III and Empress Eugénie. She became Empress of India, placing her at the head of the largest colonial empire since that of Charles V. A symbol of the British Empire, at its height she ruled over a quarter of the world.

Above:
Edwin Landseer,
Queen Victoria at Osborne, 1867.

Facing page:
Heinrich von Angeli, *Queen Victoria of Great Britain*, 1899.

EMMELINE PANKHURST

(1858–1928)

In 1999, *Time* magazine placed Emmeline Pankhurst—born in Manchester into a politically committed family—among the hundred most important figures of the twentieth century. Emmeline was not the only suffragette of her day, but she was one of the most remarkable.

Her interest in women's suffrage started while she was still a girl, inspired by her mother's activism. Her campaigning intensified in adulthood and became a family affair, involving her lawyer husband, Richard, and her daughters. Her controversial tactics and their effectiveness are still the subject of debate, but her intentions in favor of women's suffrage in the United Kingdom are respected. In the English-speaking world, the movement had been successful in New Zealand in 1893 and in Australia in 1902.

In the United Kingdom, the campaign for women's votes was initially peaceful, led by law-abiding suffragists such as Millicent Garrett Fawcett. Then came the "suffragettes," who opted for disruption, civil disobedience, and ultimately violence: among them, Emmeline and two of her daughters, Christabel and Sylvia. In 1903, they founded the Women's Social and Political Union (WSPU). The suffragettes deliberately disturbed the peace:

they broke windows, defaced monuments, cut telegraph wires, committed arson, and even hurled bombs. The first WSPU martyr came in 1913, when Emily Davison fell under the hooves of a racehorse belonging to King George V. Not everyone who campaigned for women's votes agreed with the suffragettes' methods. In 1907, the Women's Freedom League was founded by those who rejected vandalism. Emmeline's authoritarian nature, too, had discouraged some, and alienated her daughters Adela and, later, Sylvia.

Emmeline was arrested five times between 1908 and 1913. When in prison, suffragettes went on hunger strike in protest, and they were brutally force-fed. Emmeline's imprisonment prompted high-profile protests from her supporters, including, in 1914, the slashing of Velázquez's painting *The Rokeby Venus*, in the National Gallery in London, by Mary Richardson.

In 1918, female property owners over the age of thirty obtained the right to vote in the United Kingdom. One month after Emmeline's death, in June 1928, this right was extended to all women over the age of twenty-one.

Emmeline Pankhurst arrested
and led away by a policeman
after attempting to present a petition
to King George V at Buckingham Palace,
on June 2, 1914.

LOUISE WEISS

(1893–1983)

On July 17, 1979, the opening address at the first session of the European Parliament in Strasbourg was given by its oldest member, Louise Weiss, affectionately known as the "grandmother of Europe."

Born into a Jewish-Protestant family and the eldest of six children, in 1914 Louise took the *agrégation* exam—the extremely competitive exam for higher education teachers. She was one of only 10 percent of women to pass the exam, and the youngest, but she kept this success a secret from her father, a Corps des Mines engineer, who did not think girls should have an education.

When World War I broke out, she worked as a nurse—an experience that affected her greatly, and led to her interest in working toward international peace. After the war, she became a journalist. She wrote for *L'Europe Nouvelle*, a journal devoted to the idea of a European confederation rooted in humanism and culture and to overcoming nationalistic rivalries. To her eyes, the Treaty of Versailles, by humiliating Germany, portended a bad omen. Initially in favor of the League of Nations, in 1930 she opened her "School for Peace," a think tank attended by notable speechmakers.

Her faith in the League of Nations was lost when Hitler took power in 1933. With it went her support of appeasement. She left *L'Europe Nouvelle* and directed her efforts to the struggle for women's suffrage, founding a new organization, La Femme Nouvelle. In order to gain attention for the cause, she took part in a number of high-profile stunts: as a protest, she stood

symbolically as a candidate for the 5ème arrondissement in Paris in the legislative elections of 1936, transforming hatboxes into dummy ballot boxes. She held noisy meetings in cafés, a predominantly male domain; when stopped by policemen, she threw rice powder over them; with other suffragettes, she ran onto the racecourse at Longchamp.

During World War II, she edited a Resistance newspaper, in hiding. After the Liberation, she supported university peace research institutions and then started traveling to make documentaries. Keen to leave a record of her political ideas and commitment, she wrote novels, plays, essays, and a six-volume autobiography.

In 1979, she ran for the European Parliament, and became its oldest elected member. She received many awards for her work, including Grand Officer of the Legion of Honor.

Above:
Louise Weiss (top row, third from left) surrounded by women's suffrage activists, 1936.

Facing page:
Louise Weiss in 1935.

MARGARET THATCHER

(1925–2013)

Who was this "tigress surrounded by hamsters," as described by historian and academic Peter Hennessy? Who was this woman who made her ministers queasy with terror when she sat down and opened her famous handbag?

Clearly brilliant, Margaret Thatcher—later Baroness Thatcher—did not emerge from one of the customary seedbeds of British statecraft. First a chemist, then a lawyer, this daughter of a grocer and a seamstress was appointed Secretary of State for Education and Science in the government of Edward Heath. The first woman to lead the Conservative Party (1975–1990), she was also the first female prime minister of the United Kingdom (1979–1990), winning a majority three times.

Still a controversial figure today, Margaret Thatcher was characterized by a dearth of humor and a refusal to engage in dialogue, considering it a waste of time. She knew what she wanted and rejected discussion and compromise.

Her view on entering politics was that socialism, which had prevailed since the end of World War II, had pushed Britain to the brink of economic and political collapse. Fearful of the Soviet menace, she believed that membership of Europe should be limited to the single market. In 1981, she looked on unflinchingly as IRA prisoners went on hunger strike (ten perished). In 1982, after victory in the Falklands, she was free to embark on wholesale privatization, and to lower direct taxation, abolish subsidies to universities, and crush the trade unions, such as that of the miners in 1984–85.

Despite her extreme unpopularity, she pursued radical reforms. Her conservative revolution revolved around the financial deregulation of 1986—the "Big Bang" that created a new moneyed class and turned the City of London into an even more global trading hub.

She was driven out by a plot among the party's gray suits, but the Iron Lady's ideas made something of a comeback in the late 1990s/2000s in the form of Tony Blair's Third Way.

Margaret Thatcher
on the campaign trail in 1987.

ELIZABETH II

(born 1926)

Although today Queen Elizabeth II is the symbol of Great Britain in the eyes of the world, her reign has not been a smooth one. It has seen the loss of colonies, the Cold War, and globalization, not to mention the internal pop cultural revolutions beginning in the 1960s, Margaret Thatcher's neo-liberalism, and the interminable Brexit crisis.

Criticism of the monarchy reached fever pitch in 1997, on the death of the Princess of Wales, but since then the Golden and then Diamond Jubilees (fifty and sixty years of reign) in 2002 and 2012 have confirmed the queen's immense popularity among her subjects. It seems she has emerged unscathed from all of these crises, thanks to a conservatism that is both personal and inherent to a function that, to the delight of the international press, brings with it a pomp and circumstance worthy of Louis XIV.

Much remains private in her amply documented life. She was profoundly marked by the abdication of her uncle, Edward VIII, and the unexpected accession to the throne of her father, George VI. During World War II, she served in the Auxiliary Territorial Service, where, training as a mechanic, she learned to dismantle and repair engines and drove ambulances, all the while conscious that she would be the next sovereign. Famously, and with their father's permission, she and her sister left the palace on the evening of May 8, 1945, to walk through London as the city celebrated victory over Hitler.

At the end of the war, she married Philip of Greece, her cousin with whom she was in love, forcing the union on her family. Photos taken on her early travels show her young and carefree, before royal responsibilities froze her into her trademark unflappability.

Crowned queen at the age of twenty-five, she has devoted herself entirely to the office of sovereign imposed on her by God. Brief moments of relaxation take place with her husband, her horses, her corgis, and her children and grandchildren. And she has already beaten Victoria's record (see p. 82) as the longest reigning monarch.

Sir Cecil Beaton,
Queen Elizabeth II in Coronation Robes,
1953.

SIMONE VEIL

(1927–2017)

Simone Jacob started life in sunny Nice—a pampered little girl from a secular Jewish family. There, the initial effects of war and the Occupation were not especially noticeable. Nice started out in the Zone Libre, though it was later to be occupied by the Italians. Her world was turned upside down in 1944, when, at the age of seventeen, she was arrested carrying forged papers and dispatched to the camp of Drancy with her family. On April 15, she arrived with her mother and one of her sisters at Auschwitz-Birkenau, where she was imprisoned for thirteen months, subject to hard labor.

There, experiencing hunger, disease, and humiliation, she forged a courage that would never leave her. As the Red Army advanced, the Germans attempted to conceal their crimes by dragging their prisoners from camp to camp: forty miles on foot to Gleiwitz, then eight days by train without food or water between Mauthausen, Buchenwald, and Bergen-Belsen, where her mother died.

Regaining freedom was also painful. The camp survivors were objects of terror: no one wanted to know what they had been through, and undercurrents of antisemitism were just below the surface. Simone nevertheless resumed her studies, determined to find "a real job," as her mother, who had suffered from a lack of financial independence, called it. While studying political science, she met her husband-to-be, Antoine Veil, and went on to enter the judiciary.

In 1974, under President Giscard d'Estaing, she was appointed minister of health. She was given responsibility for and channeled all her energies into pushing through the law decriminalizing abortion—and in the process became an icon in the fight against sex discrimination.

Five years later, she was elected the first president of the European Parliament, where her determination and high standards made a lasting impression. She was later appointed minister of state and then minister of social affairs, health, and urban affairs in the government of Édouard Balladur.

She was elected to the Académie Française in 2008. In 2010, a survey ranked her France's favorite woman. On July 1, 2018, a year after her death, Simone Veil was reinterred in the Pantheon in Paris—one of only five women to be so honored—together with her husband.

Simone Veil when minister of health, c. 1975.

ANGELA MERKEL

(born 1954)

There is a paradox in Angela Merkel's childhood: at the time that thousands of East Germans were streaming westwards, her parents set out from Hamburg in the opposite direction. Her father, a Lutheran pastor, wanted to be where he thought he would be most useful. As a child, Angela soon realized that, if she wanted to fit in, she would have to compromise. So, for a social life, she joined the FDJ (German Free Youth), remaining a member until the fall of the Berlin Wall. To avoid indoctrination, she studied physics and chemistry—hard sciences over which political ideology has little influence. Awarded a PhD in 1986, her stance is that of a Protestant intellectual wary of ideology and convinced that people should behave in a conscientious, reasonable, compassionate, and pragmatic manner.

Angela had long perceived that the GDR would destroy itself due to its economic weaknesses, and the fall of the wall confirmed this in her eyes. She kicked off her political career as spokesperson for Lothar de Maizière: the first, and last, democratically elected head of the GDR. Joining the Christian Democratic Union, she then became a member of the Bundestag. She was twice appointed federal minister by Helmut Kohl. In 2000, she was elected chair of the CDU, and was reelected regularly until 2016.

On October 10, 2005, she was elected chancellor with a coalition government, a post she still holds. She is the first woman to hold this office in Germany, as well as the youngest—she was fifty-one when she came to power. A champion of "political balancing acts," she embodies Germany—she is widely known as "Mutti Merkel" (Mommy Merkel)—and has carved out a position as the leader of Europe, representing the nations of the north.

Forbes magazine has named her the most powerful woman in the world thirteen times, but Greece's problems in 2009 and the migrant crisis of 2015 brought seismic changes. Today, she has no obvious successor, and the extreme right continues its rise.

Angela Merkel in Berlin in 2013.

NORDIC WOMEN LEADERS

The Nordic nations have a very impressive record. Four of the five countries—Sweden is the exception—have elected women as heads of state.

In Finland, Tarja Halonen became the first female president of the republic in 2000. Today the country is led by a coalition of five parties, all of them headed by women—and young ones to boot: four are under thirty-five, while the current president, Sanna Marin, is the youngest government leader in the world, at just thirty-four years of age.

In Iceland, Vigdis Finnbogadóttir became president in 1980—the first woman head of state in a democratic country—and was reelected in 1984, 1988, and 1992. She currently dedicates her work to women's rights around the world. As for Jóhanna Sigurðardóttir, she held important positions (minister of social affairs and social security) from 1987 to 2009, when she became prime minister. The first openly homosexual head of government, she was succeeded in the post in 2017 by Katrín Jakobsdóttir, an environmentalist, feminist, and anti-militarist.

In Norway, the most famous woman politician is Gro Harlem Brundtland, who became prime minister in 1981. A physician, this feminist studied in her own country and at Harvard. Minister of the environment in 1974, she was appointed head of the Social Democrat government in 1981, remaining in the post until 1996. A pioneer of sustainable development, she headed the WHO from 1998 to 2003. Norway is also where minister of transport Ketil Solvik-Olsen stepped down to further the medical career of his wife.

In Denmark, Mette Frederiksen, elected Social Democrat MP at the age of twenty-four, was appointed minister of employment and later minister of justice in the coalition government of Helle Thorning-Schmidt—another remarkable woman—then party leader in 2015, and prime minister in 2019.

As for Sweden, it may not—as yet—have had a woman head of state, but there is strict gender parity in the government and its laws are highly favorable to women.

Clockwise, from top left:
Iceland's Vigdis Finnbogadóttir.
Norway's Gro Harlem Brundtland
in 1999.
Denmark's Mette Frederiksen in 2019.
Finland's Sanna Mirella Marin in 2019.

The Americas

The role of women in the Americas can only be understood by taking into account the unique history of these two continents. It is only five hundred years since Europeans first made landfall on American shores. Five hundred years since they started settling territories previously unknown to them and which they christened the New World. They made their land grab without scruple, chasing the original inhabitants into the most inhospitable corners, eradicating their cultures, their traditions, and their religions, calling them inferior, primitive, and pagan. From the late sixteenth century until the end of the nineteenth, with the abolition of slavery in Brazil in 1888, they brought slaves from Africa to work plantations growing crops that Europeans soon found indispensable: tobacco, sugar, and cotton. It is through this problematic prism that this story of struggle, and on which so many women left their mark, must be viewed.

In the United States, women have played a significant role in the struggle for racial equality. Rosa Parks became the face of the civil rights movement when her refusal to give up her seat on a bus to a white man led to her arrest, and ushered in a series of nationwide protests initiated by Dr. Martin Luther King, Jr. On the eve of her trial, Black Americans launched a boycott of buses in Montgomery, Alabama, and began a 381-day march, in the wake of which the Supreme Court declared bus segregation unconstitutional. And Rosa Parks was not the first. US history reveals many Black women activists and campaigners, such as Harriet Tubman, an enslaved woman from Maryland, who arranged the escape of many of her peers; Ida Wells, also an enslaved woman, who founded a newspaper in Memphis and

Above, top:
Rosa Parks sits at the front of a bus
in Montgomery, Alabama,
on December 21, 1956, after the
Supreme Court ruled segregation
on city buses illegal.

Above, bottom:
Mary McLeod Bethune,
American educator and civil rights
activist, at Daytona Beach, Florida,
in January 1943.

combated lynching across the United States; and Mary McLeod Bethune, who opened a school for Black girls. There are many others, some of whom history has overlooked, but whose contribution was no less important. White women also fought racism, including First Lady Eleanor Roosevelt and Anita Whitney, who joined the Communist Party and campaigned against the lynching of Black men accused of rape.

Native American women also became activists in the United States, like Cecilia Fire Thunder, Madonna Thunder Hawk, and Wilma Pearl Mankiller: tribal leaders striving to improve the conditions of their sisters. In Latin America, in the Amazon rainforest, Kayapó chief Raoni may be the most famous campaigner in the fight against deforestation, but a warrior woman from the same tribe has also made headlines: protesting against the Belo Monte Dam, Tuira stunned the world in 1989 when she appeared at a conference wielding a machete, swiping it in front of the speaker's cheek. With support from chiefs Raoni and Paiakan, as well as from the musician Sting, the dam works were interrupted, although not abandoned (the dam has now been in operation since 2016). Another emblematic woman from Latin America—albeit the polar opposite of Tuira—is Eva Perón, whom many Argentines still remember fondly for her generosity to the poor. A woman who started life at the very bottom of the ladder, she worked hard to make the wealthy pay.

Above, top:
Tuira demonstrating against
the dam at Belo Monte in 1989.

Above, center:
Cecilia Fire Thunder in 1994.

Above, bottom:
Wilma Pearl Mankiller on Cherokee
tribal land in Talequa, Oklahoma, undated.

POCAHONTAS

(c. 1595–1617)

Forget everything you think you know of this legendary figure—especially the Disney movie. First of all, her name wasn't Pocahontas at all, but Matoaka: "Little Snow Feather." Pocahontas was her nickname, meaning, according to one of the early colonists, "Little Wanton"— now more often thought to mean "Playful One." When the English landed in 1607 on the coast of what is now Virginia, their captain, John Smith, established a colony on the territory of the Powhatans, whose chief was Matoaka's father, Wahunsenacawh. Smith met Matoaka when he was taken prisoner while exploring to expand the colony. She was then about ten years old and he twenty-seven. According to legend, this slip of a girl braved her father's wrath to help an enemy chief. In so doing she helped bring the English and the Powhatans together, first as an intermediary, then as an interpreter.

It is believed that at the age of fourteen she married Kocoum, with whom she had a child. The marriage did not last long: kidnapped by the English, she was used as a bargaining chip against prisoners held by her father. When negotiations failed, she remained in detention not far from Jamestown, the first English colonial settlement; historians are divided on whether she was mistreated or not. It was here that John Rolfe, one of the first tobacco farmers, met and proposed to marry her.

In becoming his wife in 1614, Matoaka was forced to abandon her language, her culture, even her name; the new Mrs. Rolfe was baptized "Rebecca." A year later, a son, Thomas, was born.

Her sacrifices heralded a period of peaceful relations between the Powhatans and the English—an interlude between two savage wars. To attract new settlers to Virginia and show that the native people were not hostile, Pocahontas was sent to England as a cultural envoy. Her arrival in London with eleven members of her tribe caused a sensation, and people went in droves to see this living advertisement for colonization. Some accounts say she was presented at the court of King James I and Queen Anne, but these are disputed.

After a sojourn of a few months in the country, she fell ill in the English climate. Before she was able to return home to Virginia, Pocahontas—a legend who has both delighted and exasperated America in equal measure—died of a suspected pulmonary disease (pneumonia or tuberculosis). A statue was erected to her in Gravesend, Kent, England, where she passed away and was buried. Later, in the United States, she was commemorated with a stamp in 1907, and in 2000 she was honored by the state of Virginia for her contributions to her community.

Simon van de Passe,
engraving of Pocahontas, 1616.

MATOAKA ALS REBECCA FILIA POTENTISS PRINC POWHATANI IMP VIRGINIÆ

Ætatis suæ 21. A° 1616.

Matoaks als Rebecka daughter to the mighty Prince
Powhatan Emperour of Attanougskomouck als virginia
converted and baptized in the Christian faith, and
wife to the wortt Mr. Joh Rolff.

Si: Paß: sculp: Compton Holland excud:

SOJOURNER TRUTH

(1797–1883)

Born into slavery in Dutch-speaking New York State, Isabella Bomfree had been bought and sold four times by the time she was a teenager. Forced into marriage, she had five children. The year before New York State abolished slavery in 1827, Belle—as she was known—and her infant daughter left her fourth master for New York City. When, the following year, her five-year-old son was illegally sold in Alabama, she dared to go to court—the first Black woman to do so and win against a white man.

In 1843, she became a Methodist and changed her name to Sojourner Truth, describing how she had received a message from God telling her to preach the truth. She became renowned for her lectures on the abolition of slavery, on the power of women and, later, against the death penalty. Extremely charismatic and over five feet eleven inches tall, she had a commanding presence; she also possessed an attractive voice and, though illiterate, knew the Bible by heart.

Her speeches have become legendary. In Ohio in 1851, she asked the famous question, "Ain't I a woman?" attacking the invisibility of Black women. No one version of her speech remains, although the most accepted one, recorded several years after the event by an eye-witness, attempts to recreate her accent and speech patterns: "Nobody eber helps me into carriages, or ober mud-puddles.... And ain't I a woman?... Look at me! Look at my arm.... I have ploughed and planted." In Indiana in 1858, when a man in the audience heckled her, exclaiming that she wasn't a woman, she stood her ground, undaunted, and pulled off her top to prove otherwise.

In addition to touring the country to preach, she collected food for Black Union regiments during the Civil War and arranged jobs for Black soldiers after demobilization. In 1864, she met President Lincoln and later, in 1870, President Ulysses S. Grant. She campaigned tirelessly for former slaves to be given land in the west—"40 acres and a mule"—but this never came to pass, no more than her idea of a "Black State" on the same land.

When she died aged eighty-six, more than a thousand people followed her casket. In 2014, *Smithsonian* magazine voted her one of the hundred most important people in the United States.

Sojourner Truth, undated.

HARRIET TUBMAN

(c. 1820–1913)

In the Bible, Harriet preferred the Old Testament, with Moses saving God's chosen, to the New Testament, which speaks of obedience. Born into slavery in Maryland in around 1820, as a child Tubman suffered appalling physical mistreatment at the hands of white men, one day suffering such a severe head injury that it left her with terrible aftereffects for the rest of her life: dizziness, pain, and epileptic seizures, as well as what she believed were visions announcing the Word of God.

In 1849, in her late twenties, she escaped to Philadelphia by the Underground Railroad, a network of safe houses run by abolitionist activists, often Quakers. On crossing the Mason-Dixon Line dividing the South from the North, she recalled, "I looked at my hands to see if I was the same person."

She started earning her livelihood in Philadelphia, but almost immediately returned to Maryland to bring her family north. In eleven years, and over some thirteen missions, she managed to escort all of her family and then other enslaved people—around seventy in all, although some say as many as two hundred—to freedom. She was smart, preferring to travel in winter to avoid detection, and on Saturdays, so that the breakout would only appear in the newspapers on the following Monday. Her various ruses included acting insane or adopting disguises, and, in case of an alert, she would even carry around chickens, which she would let loose and chase after. No doubt, her appearance also helped her to avoid detection; no one expected this tiny woman with disabilities to be the mastermind behind so many daring—and dangerous—escapes. She became known as Moses, as she led her people to freedom, and it was said of her that "she never lost a passenger."

In 1861, at the outbreak of the Civil War, Harriet worked as a spy, scout, and nurse on the Union side, treating dysentery-stricken troops with herbs. She also acted as a guide through the swamps of South Carolina. She was the first woman to head an assault with the army of the North on the Combahee River at Port Royal, rescuing seven hundred and fifty enslaved people. She repeated the same feat at the battle at Fort Wagner.

After the war, she joined the movement for women's suffrage. When asked if women should have the vote, she replied, "I suffered enough to believe it." Despite the hardships of her life and her apparent physical frailty, Tubman lived until her nineties, when she died in abject poverty, of pneumonia, in 1913.

Harriet Tubman, c. 1890.

ELEANOR ROOSEVELT

(1884–1962)

Eleanor Roosevelt was born into a well-connected world of privilege—with an Upper East Side apartment with servants and a manor on the Hudson River—but her early years were tragic. Her beautiful mother died at twenty-eight and her beloved father at thirty-two, addicted to alcohol and drugs. Shy and hung up about her appearance, she found solace under the wing of her French headmistress, Mademoiselle Souvestre, during her years at a boarding school in England.

Niece of former US president Theodore Roosevelt, she married a distant cousin, Franklin Delano, who was also a Roosevelt and who, too, would become a US president. Her marriage was not easy. Living under the shadow of her domineering mother-in-law and betrayed by her husband's infidelity, she agreed to remain with him only to help him advance his political career. But in so doing she began to forge her own path.

In 1921, when Franklin D. Roosevelt was paralyzed by what is now suspected to have been Guillain-Barré syndrome, Eleanor made public appearances on his behalf and persuaded him to stay in politics. He was elected governor in 1928, just before the Wall Street crash. She, meanwhile, pursued issues in her own right, getting involved in the Women's Trade Union League and teaching in a girls' school. She developed friendships with women, including aviator Amelia Earhart.

When FDR became president of the United States in 1933, Eleanor was initially dismayed at taking on the role of First Lady—one that traditionally focused on domestic issues—but she used it as a launching pad to a new life. Raising the profile of the position—which she held longer than any other First Lady in US history—she gave it a political role, directing the social aspects of her husband's New Deal toward women, the poor, Black Americans, and refugees.

Through her newspaper articles, talks, and radio appearances she enhanced the couple's popularity, but she herself attracted controversy. In her treatment of many issues, she was consistently ahead of her time, particularly regarding racial and gender equality. She was one of the few voices to criticize the New Deal on the grounds that funds were not shared equally among all races, particularly in the segregated southern states. After the death of her husband, she remained devoted to social issues throughout her life. She was appointed as a delegate to the United Nations General Assembly in 1946 and went on to serve as the first chairperson of the Commission on Human Rights. She played an instrumental role in drafting the Universal Declaration of Human Rights, and President Harry S. Truman referred to her as "the First Lady of the world." When she died in 1962, the *New York Times* described her as "the object of almost universal respect."

Eleanor Roosevelt,
on her sixty-sixth birthday,
at Lake Success, New York,
October 11, 1950.

EVA PERÓN

(1919–1952)

It was June 1947 and Madrid was suffocating in the summer heat. To the astonishment of the crowd, Eva Perón stepped out in mink. She was on an official visit to Franco's Spain and had arrived on a private plane, with another reserved exclusively for her wardrobe of two hundred outfits. She was on a mission to bewitch Europe as successfully as she had dazzled Argentina.

Eva was the illegitimate daughter of a landowner from the province of Buenos Aires. From youth, she was motivated by a desire to better herself, and to avenge social injustices. She was ambitious, working her way from prostitution to minor roles in a radio series. It was through radio that she first made her name and, as she rose to political prominence, she would use it to forge her extraordinary legend. With her provincial accent and impassioned speeches, she became an idol of the Argentine people, who saw her as one of their own.

In 1944, Eva met Colonel Juan Domingo Perón, minister of war and labor secretary, who became vice-president that year. The couple often hit the headlines, helped by Eva's camera-friendly, bleached-blonde, American starlet look. She was soon taking the reins. More courageous than her husband, she was sincere in speaking to the poorest of the poor—the *descamisados*—and it was thanks to her that Juan rose to head the country as president in 1946.

Their image is engraved forever in Argentine hearts. More than three million portraits, seven million postcards, and fourteen million booklets of the couple were distributed. Young children learned to read, "Evita is our beloved mother!" When out among the poor, this charismatic woman listened to their complaints and gave them whatever she thought useful, from dentures and sewing machines to housing. She built dispensaries, hospitals, and homes for young girls, for orphans, and for the elderly. She even had a nine-carriage "hospital train" built, which would crisscross the country and serve the remotest towns. But in order to realize these projects, she often resorted to acts verging on extortion, and, as a result, she was both idolized and loathed.

Deaf to advice, she followed her path undeterred, until her death from cancer at the age of thirty-three. Eva Perón—known as the "Angel," the "Good Fairy," the "Sweet," the "Pure," "Santa Evita"—left her country inconsolable.

Numa Ayrinhac, *The President of Argentina, Juan Domingo Perón, with His Wife Eva (Evita)*, 1949.

ANGELA DAVIS

(born 1944)

An icon of the 1960s and 1970s, Angela Davis stood at the forefront of US politics for many years, arousing strong reactions, both positive and negative. She was born in Birmingham, Alabama, into a family of civil rights activists. At a young age, she accompanied her mother on demonstrations and became aware of the Ku Klux Klan's bombings of Black homes in a neighborhood that earned the moniker "Dynamite City." In segregated Birmingham, she attended a school for Black children. Shocked and angered by schoolbooks promoting anti-poor and racist sentiment, she naturally turned to politics. As a student at Brandeis University, she read Jean-Paul Sartre, and then studied at the University of Frankfurt, under Herbert Marcuse. On returning to the United States, she joined the Black-only section of the Communist Party, the Che-Lumumba Club.

A philosophy professor at the University of California, Angela Davis quickly became known as a radical feminist activist, member of the Communist Party USA, and sympathizer of the Black Panthers. Ronald Reagan, California state governor at the time, arranged to have her fired in 1968. Following a courtroom hostage-taking in Marin County, California that left four people dead, she became one of the FBI's Ten Most Wanted: she had bought one of the weapons used. Her arrest and imprisonment provoked a wave of protest around the world. After a year in prison, she was acquitted by a white jury.

On her release, she resumed her radical speeches against the Vietnam War and racism, but also against the penitentiary system, private prisons, and capital punishment. In 1972, she visited Cuba and the USSR, and received the Lenin Peace Prize in 1978.

Like all strong personalities, she could also make missteps. Refusing to support detainees in Czechoslovakia ("they deserve what they get"), she called those imprisoned in the USSR "Zionist fascists," for which she was lambasted by Russian writer Alexander Solzhenitsyn. She quit the Communist Party in 1991, founding the Committees of Correspondence for Democracy and Socialism.

Continuing her writing, campaigning, and public speaking, she has pursued an academic career that encourages critical thinking as a way to address and solve social injustice. Her activism has made her a cultural icon as much as a political one, and over the decades she has been referenced (along with her famous hairstyle) in songs, plays, and films—in 2018, her face was even printed on a Prada T-shirt.

Facing page:
Angela Davis at a press conference in 1969.

Pages 114–15:
Angela Davis at a rally against the death penalty in Raleigh, North Carolina, July 4, 1974.

HILLARY RODHAM CLINTON

(born 1947)

As an honor student in high school, Hillary Rodham ran for class president, losing to a boy who told her she was "stupid" for thinking a girl could be elected president. At twenty-two—upon earning her political science degree from Wellesley College—she was featured in *Life* magazine with an excerpt from her commencement speech. Her fellow students were already suggesting she could become the first woman president of the United States.

At Yale Law School, she was on the board of the *Yale Review of Social Action* and became involved in child welfare and migrant workers' issues. She was brilliant, determined, and intimidating. It was also here that fellow law student Bill Clinton caught her eye. He, too, was bowled over by her intellect, but it would take the southern charmer several attempts before she agreed to marry him.

Following Bill to his home state of Arkansas, Hillary taught law at the university. When he was elected governor in 1976, she became First Lady of the state, with a passionate commitment to family, education, and health care. In 1993, when Hillary entered the White House with Bill, the latter quipped that the country was getting "two for the price of one." However, her failure to push through healthcare reform saw her sidelined to the role of "wife of." When she stood by her husband during the Monica Lewinsky affair, she was criticized from all sides. She polished her image and went on to be elected New York state senator in 2000.

In 2008, she made a bid for the Democratic presidential nomination but was narrowly defeated. When Barack Obama became president, he appointed her secretary of state. Her approach to foreign affairs, seen by many as hawkish, was characterized by what she called "smart power": a combination of hard power and diplomacy. She sought to empower women and girls around the world, seeing a direct correlation between a nation's instability and gender inequality. By the time she left her post as head of US diplomacy, she had clocked up almost one million air miles and visited 112 countries.

In 2016, Hillary Clinton became the first woman to be nominated by a major political party when she won the Democratic primary. She then won the popular vote by 3 million but lost the electoral college to Donald Trump.

Hillary Clinton remains a controversial figure. She has her many supporters, but she has also struggled to gain public popularity. Her public image seems contradictory: many consider her elitist, arrogant, or a lefty, while for others she is not progressive enough, if her views on the death penalty or divorce laws are taken into account. What is certain is that she leaves no one indifferent; in US politics, no woman looms as large.

Hillary Clinton on the campaign trail in Miami, October 11, 2016.

DILMA ROUSSEFF

(born 1947)

Does Dilma Rousseff, the most unpopular president in the history of Brazil, deserve such opprobrium? Or is this nation—which appears, on the surface, to be so laid-back—just as profoundly macho as many others in Latin America?

The springboard for Rousseff's political career was her time as a guerrilla under the military dictatorship: captured in 1970, she was tortured for twenty-two days and imprisoned for three years. Clearly, she was unafraid to risk her life for her principles, and after her release from prison she and her husband helped to found the Democratic Labor Party. Subsequently, this economist was spotted by Luiz Inácio Lula da Silva who became her mentor, making her his energy policy adviser in 2002, then minister of energy when he won the election, and chief of staff from 2005 to 2010.

In preparation for the 2011 presidential elections, in a nation poised to become the world's epicenter for plastic surgery, Rousseff herself felt pressure to go under the knife as part of a pre-election makeover—would the same ever be expected of her male counterparts? Her campaign was backed by Lula, buoyed up by a popularity rate of 80 percent, thanks to a boom that had lifted 24 million Brazilians out of poverty since 2003; in 2009 alone, 1.7 million jobs were created—a side effect of off-shoring.

At sixty-two, she became the first woman to be elected president in Brazil, and upon taking office she appointed six women ministers and two others to key posts—an unprecedented move, even considering Michelle Bachelet in Chile, Violeta Chamorro in Nicaragua, and Cristina Kirchner in Argentina. According to *Forbes*, in 2011 and 2012 she was the third most powerful woman in the world, rising to second in 2013. In 2014, she was reelected by a narrow margin.

But then came the fall. An economic slump hit and unemployment soared. In 2015, the left-wing coalition was accused of taking kickbacks on contracts overcharged to the state company Petrobras. Rousseff was not mentioned specifically, although she was accused of doctoring accounts to conceal the public deficit. Her popularity plummeted to 10 percent, and the right-wing media, controlled by six leading families, pushed for her impeachment. On the left, she was blamed for failing to halt dam projects in the Amazon. She was impeached on August 31, 2016.

Dilma Rousseff at a conference
at the Sorbonne University, Paris,
on September 17, 2019.

NATIVE AMERICAN WARRIOR WOMEN

Historically, Native American societies have been more egalitarian than European ones, yet European history has overlooked these achievements. Weetamo, queen of the Wampanoags in the seventeenth century; Dahteste (1860–1955), an Apache warrior woman; or, more recently, Deb Haaland and Sharice Davides, the first two Native American women elected to the US Congress, are not household names.

They are not the only indigenous American women worthy of note. Cecilia Fire Thunder, first woman tribal leader of the Oglala Sioux, has campaigned ceaselessly for native women's reproductive rights and healthcare. In 1960, her family was removed, like others, from her reserve in Pine Ridge, South Dakota, to Los Angeles, more than 1,200 miles away. There, Cecilia studied nursing, working for twenty years in a clinic for Native Americans. Returning to her people in 1986, she became involved in combating domestic violence and alcoholism in her community. (An estimated one-third of Native American women are victims of rape, and many babies are born with fetal alcohol syndrome.) She also sought to promote the Lakota language and culture, to instill pride in her community. In 2004, the year Cecilia Fire Thunder became leader, the state of South Dakota proposed to outlaw abortion completely; she promptly built a clinic on the reserve, but the Tribal Council declared that she had outstripped her powers and removed her as leader in 2006. Having become a high-profile figure, she continued to campaign against the anti-abortion law, which would be rejected eventually, and today she campaigns and speaks regularly on issues relating to women's reproductive rights and native women.

Another remarkable Native American woman is Wilma Pearl Mankiller (1945–2010), who was principal chief of the Cherokee, the second largest Nation in the United States, for ten years. In 1964, her political awareness was raised in the course of the occupation of Alcatraz prison in San Francisco Bay. As a health activist, she founded a clinic and a mobile eye-care unit. Her efforts resulted in a decline in infant mortality, improved education, and a twofold increase in jobs.

The grande dame of these warrior women is Madonna Thunder Hawk, who, in her eighties, continues a life of protest and campaigning to improve the lives of her people, particularly women. She was active in the movement against the Dakota Access Pipeline, which transported oil through sacred sites and threatened sources of drinking water. In March 2020, a district judge ruled that the US government had not sufficiently investigated the environmental and human impact of the pipeline and ordered it to be shut down, pending the results of an environmental review.

Madonna Thunder Hawk
in a photograph taken for the promotion
of the film *Warrior Women*, 2018.

Asia
Pacific

Official portrait of Empress
Dowager Cixi by Chinese court
photographer Yu Xunling, c. 1895.

Post-colonial Asia is the first region in the world where women were elected to positions of supreme power—although not all of them have turned out to be role models.

In the West, Sri Lanka has always had something of a magical reputation. It was where Sinbad's adventures were set, under the name of the island of Serendip, in *The Thousand and One Nights*. This island is also where, in 1960, Sirimavo Bandaranaike became the first woman in contemporary history to be elected to head a government. Born into a prestigious family, in 1940 she married Solomon Bandaranaike, who was assassinated in 1959 while prime minister of what was then Ceylon. The following year, Sirimavo became leader of the Freedom Party, before herself being elected prime minister at the age of forty-four. Returning to office in 1970 and again in 1994, it was she who steered through Parliament the proclamation of the republic by which Ceylon became Sri Lanka. Although nicknamed "the Weeping Widow" because she tended to cry easily, her political opinions were strong. Nationalizing banking, insurance, and oil, she also made approaches to India, the USSR, and Mao's China. Her most glaring failure? The Tamil question that degenerated into civil war. She nonetheless holds the record for prime ministerial longevity: three terms of office totaling eighteen years.

The region has also seen the emergence of other female politicians: Sirimavo Bandaranaike's own daughter, Chandrika Kumaratunga, became prime minister in 1994, before being elected president that same year and appointing her mother as prime minister. Like Sirimavo before her, she was unable to solve the Tamil problem and even lost an eye during an assassination attempt by the Tigers.

Above, top:
Sirimavo Bandaranaike
during a speech at the United Nations
General Assembly in 1976.

Above, bottom:
Chandrika Kumaratunga,
Sirimavo Bandaranaike's daughter,
when president of Sri Lanka, in 2001.

Having former heads of state in the family seems to be an advantage in these women's pursuit of powerful positions: even globally recognized political icons such as Indira Gandhi and Benazir Bhutto were daughters of previous leaders.

In Bangladesh, Khaleda Zia, widow of the assassinated General Zia, replaced him as head of the Conservative Party, becoming the nation's first woman prime minister in 1981. Accused of corruption and embezzlement in 2006, she had been ranked by *Forbes* magazine as the thirty-third most powerful woman in the world. Her great rival was Sheikh Hasina, daughter of Bangladesh's first president, Sheikh Mujibur Rahman, who was killed in a coup in 1975. She, too, became prime minister, before being charged with extortion.

In the Philippines, Gloria Macapagal Arroyo, daughter of former president Diosdado Macapagal, was appointed undersecretary of the Department of Trade and Industry by Cory Aquino—herself a "wife of"—before assuming the presidency in 2001. Her tenure was marred by suspicions of corruption and electoral fraud.

More recently, Park Geun-hye—daughter of military dictator Park Chung-hee, who ruled the country from 1966 to 1979, when he was assassinated—was president of South Korea from 2013 to 2017. She is currently serving a thirty-two-year prison sentence for abuse of power, corruption, and coercion.

Is there really so much corruption? In countries where the separation of powers is blurred, accusations of corruption are an expedient way to eliminate political opponents. This classic political weapon is deployed in many regions of the globe, especially against powerful women.

Above, top:
Khaleda Zia on the campaign trail in 1991.

Above, center:
Gloria Macapagal Arroyo, president of the Philippines, talking to the press in 2008.

Above, bottom:
Park Geun-hye, president of South Korea, in Seoul in 2015.

EMPRESS JINGU

(169–269)

Once upon a time, there was a legendary empress consort of Japan called Okinaga-tarashi-hime, better known by her posthumous Chinese name, Jingu. A daughter of the aristocracy, she learned to wield the *naginata* (spear) and *kaiten* (dagger), as well as mastering the art of *tantojutsu*, fighting with a special curved knife. In short, she was an *onna bugeisha*—the female equivalent of a samurai.

Jingu was the wife of Emperor Chuai. When Chuai decided to take on the Kumaso rebels on the island of Kyushu, Jingu asked him to postpone the expedition, in order to wage war on Shiraki, today's Korea. Possessed by deities who spoke through her, Jingu told him of a land to the west, full of gold and silver and other dazzling treasures. Ignoring her predictions and spurning the gods' warnings, the emperor died in 209, while playing the *koto*—a type of plucked zither—at the Kashihi palace.

Jingu, now with child, pulled on her armor and set out to conquer Korea herself. According to one account of her legend, thanks to help from the magical jewels of the god Ryujin and Sun goddess Amaterasu, she triumphed without shedding a drop of blood. Crossing an inland sea, a giant buffalo emerged from the waves and attacked her. The god Sumiyoshi appeared in the form of an old man, grabbed the animal by the horns, and hurled him into oblivion.

The conquest of the three kingdoms of Korea took three years, with Jingu returning just in time to give birth to Ojin, whom she kept in her womb throughout the campaign. To prevent the baby from being born too early, some say that she hung rocks around her waist; others claim that she even pushed the stones inside her to prevent the baby from being born. Crushing revolts by the sons of Chuai—the princes Kagoraka and Oshikuma—Jingu ruled as regent for sixty years, until, in 269, her son ascended the throne.

This legendary empress is the only woman to appear on a Japanese banknote, and even a Tokyo subway station bears her name.

Facing page:
Utagawa Kuniyoshi,
Return of the Boats at Tsukushi
(Empress Jingu watching for the return
of her victorious fleet of ships
from Korea), c. 1842–43.

Pages 128–29:
Tsukioka Yoshitoshi,
*Concise Illustrated History
of Great Japan: Empress Jingu
Leading the Invasion of Korea*, 1879.

武内宿禰

明治十二年四月

九屋町五番地

畫工 月岡米次郎 出板人 森本順三

武則天

WU ZETIAN

(c. 625–705)

We are familiar today with the horsewomen of the Tang period through the distinctive terra-cotta figures of that period—rosy-cheeked, with a doll-like silhouette and their hair tied in a bun, they are mounted on horses to display their riding prowess. Wu Zetian was one of them. Packed off to join the harem of Emperor Taizong, she was soon noticed for her impressive understanding of horses.

Against all expectations, after serving Taizong for ten years, she managed to avoid ending her days in a monastery by currying favor with his successor, Gaozong. But that was just the beginning: she plotted to eliminate the empress consort and the chief concubine, strangling her own young daughter to implicate them in her murder. Disappointed by the emperor's lackluster reaction, she went on to accuse her rivals of practicing black magic and devised ghastly tortures as punishment: after a hundred strokes of the cane, they were dismembered, and left to die in a jar of fermenting rice wine.

From that point, she was unstoppable. Empress by 655, her word was law, and she meted out justice and the right to life and death. Her politics, however, were steeped in Taoism and revealed unexpected humanity: tax cuts in support of farming and sericulture, edicts in favor of women's rights, reductions in the duration of bonded labor, abolition of compulsory military service, among others. She also introduced competitive examinations for recruiting mandarins.

Violence and intrigue were never far away: Gaozong died in suspicious circumstances, and the couple's two eldest sons, who were popular, were murdered. The last two offspring were spared a similar fate, as they were considered stupid, which allowed Wu to hold on to power. Concocting a prestigious genealogy for herself, in 690 she took the title "Holy and Divine Sovereign Emperor," triggering a revolt among the princes of the blood, which she quashed with the ruthlessness that characterized her whole life. After a reign of twenty-two years, she was forced to abdicate. However, even in death, her ghost was so feared that her will was executed to the letter.

Wu Zetian remains the only empress regnant in the whole of Chinese history. Paradoxically, centuries later Mao Zedong's wife would be dubbed "the new Wu Zetian."

Anonymous,
The Empress Wu Zetian,
eighteenth century.

RAZIA SULTAN

(1205–1240)

Born in Muslim India, Razia was raised as a boy by her father, the Mughal sultan of Delhi. Since she could ride both horse and elephant and had a head for politics, she was made his heir, at the expense of the male children whom the sultan dismissed as inept: "My sons think only of youthful pleasures and none of them possesses the qualities of a king. After I die you will see that no one will be more competent to run the state than my daughter." On the sultan's death, the emirs nevertheless rejected rule by a female and turned to one of his sons. However, before long, they were rallying to the late sultan's decision. Thus, in 1236, Razia succeeded as sultan and not "sultana" of Delhi, becoming the one and only female sultan in its history. Abandoning the veil, she adopted the turban, wore men's clothes, and carried a sword. Her opposition to every tradition shocked many to the core.

She spent much of her brief, three-and-a-half-year reign fostering the arts and overseeing projects such as laying roads, digging wells, planting trees, and building schools and libraries. But her liberalism enraged the emirs; a fierce advocate of antidiscrimination, Razia Sultan was intent on abolishing the special poll tax levied on Hindus that enshrined their second-class status.

The emirs were also infuriated by her relationship with an Abyssinian slave, Jamal ud-Din Yaqut, who was perhaps her lover and whom she appointed "Master of the Stables." A revolt ensued: Yaqut died in battle and Razia was captured and imprisoned, while a former childhood friend, Altunia, plotted to replace her with her step-brother. Some accounts say that she later married Altunia, and that together they attempted to seize back Delhi, unsuccessfully.

It is said that her taste for luxury betrayed her. Fleeing Delhi dressed in male attire, she sought refuge with a peasant, who noticed that the tunic she was wearing was encrusted with precious stones. He murdered her as she slept, chased off her horse, and buried her in his field. She was thirty-five years old.

According to the great Arab historian Ibn Battuta, the mausoleum of Razia Sultan in Delhi became a place of pilgrimage where one could obtain divine blessings.

Equestrian portrait of Razia Sultan, daughter of the Mughal sultan of Delhi, eighteenth century.

PŌMARE THE GREAT

(1813–1877)

By the time Aimata, the future Pōmare IV, was born, Tahiti was no longer the enchanting island described by French explorer Antoine de Bougainville in the previous century; it had long been in the grip of Protestant missionaries. Yet Aimata's childhood was carefree: she was allowed to play, sing, and dance, and she was fascinated by the passing ships visiting the island. It was the great age of whalers, buccaneers, and beachcombers—fortune hunters trading in pearls and sandalwood.

When she was crowned, the fourteen-year-old Aimata, now Pōmare, was determined to break with the rigorous Protestantism introduced by her father, Pōmare II, and return to the ancestral traditions within the Mamaia sect: a syncretic movement advocating neighborly love in all its forms. It was not to be, and she was forced to submit to the missionaries. Thus began her legendary reputation as a queen, who, even today, is renowned for her resistance to foreign domination.

While still a mere girl, she was forced to wed a cousin she disliked, but, in 1832, she remarried—this time to the handsomest man in the kingdom, Ariifaaite. She was twenty, he was five years younger. Together they had seven children.

History describes two Pōmares: one used her charm to defend her interests and those of her people; the other was a woman of infinite dignity. One wore the traditional pareu—a cloth wrap-around skirt—and sticks of gardenia behind her ear; the other dressed in a European-style silk gown (though, truth be told, she was never at ease in shoes). In later years, she adopted missionary garb: a kind of shapeless sack allowing the wearer to dispense with a corset.

Opposed, like Ranavalona III in Madagascar, to her country being a protectorate of France, Pōmare IV suffered defeat in 1846 in the Franco-Tahitian war. Relations improved with the ascent to power of Napoleon III, who treated her with deference. Retaining her position as head of state, at each opening of the assembly she was hailed with a twenty-one gun salute. Pōmare dealt with domestic affairs, under the watchful eye of the governor.

By the time she died in 1877, she had become the symbol of Tahitian identity, like Queen Victoria in Britain (see p. 82). Three years after her death, the monarchy was abolished and Tahiti became a French colony, administered directly from Paris.

Charles Giraud,
Queen Pōmare IV of Tahiti,
nineteenth century.

LAKSHMI BAI

(c. 1828–1858)

For the British, Lakshmi Bai is the Indian Joan of Arc (see p. 53): a woman prepared to sacrifice her life to drive the colonizers from her land, the kingdom of Jhansi. Raised among boys, she learned to ride both horse and elephant. She was also a born fighter. At the age of fourteen, she married the maharajah of Jhansi, who was thirty years her senior. Just nineteen at the time of her husband's death, she learned that the British proposed to annex the country. Mounting a defense, she appealed to London, but to no avail. She joined the revolt of the sepoys—Hindu and Muslim soldiers of the British army—against the East India Company. Extending to the northern and central provinces, this rebellion was considered the first phase of India's war of independence.

Lakshmi Bai trained an army of fourteen thousand volunteers, leading them into battle herself. After a lengthy siege of Jhansi during which her female recruits carried ammunition, kept watch, and supplied the soldiers with water and food, the city finally fell. Fleeing on horseback, she seized the fortress of Gwalior, one of the most strategic strongholds in all India. Despite exceptional courage and determination, however, her resistance lasted a mere three months.

A symbol of anti-colonialism, Rani Lakshmi Bai is often portrayed wearing a strange outfit that seems half-warrior half-queen: either in "pajamas," coat, and turban, carrying a sword set with precious stones; or in jodhpurs, silk blouse, low-cut corset, and a loose turban, her fingers laden with diamonds.

Legend has it that she died in men's clothes, the reins of her thoroughbred between her teeth, a sword in each hand, and a gorgeous pearl necklace around her neck. General Sir Hugh Rose, who fought against her, said of her, "Although she was a lady, she was the bravest and best military leader of the rebels. A man among mutineers."

Today, equestrian statues of her stand in many major cities across the country.

Kalighat school,
*The Mutiny of the Heroine
Rani Lakshmi Bai of Jhansi,*
nineteenth century.

CIXI

(1835–1908)

Her life began similarly to that of Wu Zetian (see p. 131): she was the concubine of a Manchu emperor, Xianfeng. But it was her seriousness and thirst for knowledge, rather than intrigue and murder, that made her stand out. Having learned to read and write, she sat at the feet of scholars and became the emperor's archivist. She gave him his first-born son, who she was determined should inherit the throne. The emperor recognized the boy as his successor, but died the very next day.

A dual regency was then established, with the official empress—known as the empress consort, who was sterile—and the empress mother, Cixi, who soon monopolized power, if only because she could read dispatches in Mandarin. Twenty years later, the empress consort died, perhaps as a result of poisoning.

At that time, poison was an effective expedient when one thinks of the one hundred and twenty dishes, plus seasonal produce, laid before Cixi at every meal. To conceal her preferences, she never took more than three spoonfuls. Three hundred people toiled away in the kitchens and a record was kept of each one responsible for washing, slicing, or seasoning the vegetables.

There was an additional rule: no one must see the empress's feet. Every day, she demanded a new pair of white silk socks, each one requiring seven to eight days' work to produce. To ensure she never ran out, three thousand seamstresses were employed to make them. Everything was codified to the point of absurdity.

But did her absolute power over the Forbidden City and its denizens extend beyond its red walls? Cut off from the world while Western powers stood at the gates, Cixi used money lent by European bankers to build a white marble ship in the middle of the gardens of the Summer Palace, instead of providing a real fleet for the Chinese military. During the Boxer Rebellion, she fled Beijing but demanded to sleep every night in a new bed—made for her by villagers—draped in coverlets of red satin.

Cixi died in 1908. Three years later, China was proclaimed a republic.

Empress Dowager Cixi
on the throne of Imperial China,
undated.

INDIRA GANDHI

(1917–1984)

Heiress to a famous Brahmin dynasty in British India, Indira Gandhi—daughter of Jawaharlal Nehru—grew up in a highly politicized family with links to Mahatma Gandhi. Her father was a leading figure in the struggle for independence and spent part of Indira's childhood in prison. Her grandfather Motilal, one of India's earliest activists, was also often behind bars. Her mother, Kamala Nehru, was an ardent feminist and she, too, was incarcerated, before dying of tuberculosis at just thirty-seven.

At the age of twelve, Indira formed the Monkey Brigade: a children's group determined to attain independence. Although her father had taught her that obligations to the homeland came first, her personal priority was to have children: the announcement of her marriage to Feroze Gandhi, a low-caste Parsi, scandalized the nation. Nonetheless, they married in 1942, and she wore a sari of rose silk spun by her father in prison. She would lend that same sari to her two daughters-in-law and, upon her death, would be cremated in it.

The year 1947 saw India's independence and the creation of Muslim Pakistan, at the cost of two million lives. Nehru became head of the government, with Indira succeeding him twenty years later—only the second woman in the world to be elected democratically to lead a country.

She was iron-willed and charismatic, and her two terms were marked by the centralization of power, as well as by a refusal to rely on foreign states. Seeking to ensure self-sufficiency in food, she launched the "green revolution." She devalued the rupee and had India join the non-aligned nations, alongside Gamal Abdel Nasser and Josip Broz Tito. In 1970, she abolished the privileges of the maharajahs, and the following year she triumphed in the third Indo-Pakistani war. She also oversaw India's rise to become the developing world's first nuclear power.

Increasingly authoritarian, she declared a state of emergency in 1975 to avoid resigning, muzzling the press and governing by decree. She also launched a vasectomy campaign: seven million were carried out in 1976, mostly on "Untouchables."

She was defeated in the 1977 elections, but returned to power three years later. In June 1984, she gave the go-ahead for the attack on the Golden Temple of Amritsar, a holy site seized by Sikh militants, which sparked a massacre. She was assassinated by her own Sikh bodyguard in October of the same year.

Indira Gandhi in 1979.

GAYATRI DEVI, MAHARANI OF JAIPUR

(1919–2009)

Her mother was the princess of Baroda and her father the prince of Cooch Behar. Gayatri Devi was raised amid the almost unimaginable luxury of the maharajahs. Her childhood was spent traveling from palace to palace in a Rolls-Royce or aboard a private train with special livery. On special occasions, meals were served on gold plates, and leisure time included tiger hunts mounted on elephants. She shot her first panther aged twelve.

Like the other women in her family, Gayatri refused to observe purdah—that cloistered life separating women from men. This set her apart from other princesses, along with a period of study that included two years in London.

In 1940, she wed Jai, maharajah of Jaipur; though she was his third wife, it was a true love match. He loved Gayatri for her looks—"one of the ten most beautiful women in the world," according to *Vogue* magazine—but also because, as a woman who traveled, could drive, and played sports, she seemed the living embodiment of his determination to rid the kingdom of purdah.

When her husband marched off to fight by the side of the British, Gayatri emerged from her passive role as an adulated queen: in 1943, she founded the Maharani Gayatri Devi Girls' School, the first state school for girls in the whole of India. Striving for the emancipation of women in Rajasthan, she led a revival in regional handicraft.

Independence in 1947 heralded the gradual abolition of the principalities. Gayatri then entered politics in the opposition Swatantra ("Independence") Party. When she ran for Parliament in 1962, she obtained a majority of 175,000 votes over the candidate for Nehru's Congress Party—the largest majority ever attained in a democratic country. Reelected five years later, she considered leaving politics after Jai's death, but was persuaded to continue.

She was fought tooth and nail by a jealous Indira Gandhi (see p. 140), who was of the opinion that there was room for only one woman in Indian politics. Indira insulted her in public, and went so far as to throw her in jail during the Emergency in 1975; Gayatri was released after 156 days, due to her fragile health. She died at the age of ninety, immensely respected in India and beyond.

Gayatri Devi, Maharani of Jaipur, undated.

BENAZIR BHUTTO

(1953–2007)

Benazir Bhutto—"the peerless," if we go by the meaning of her first name—presented an image of Islam that appeals to the West. She was attractive, educated, charismatic, gloriously elegant in her *shalwar kameez*, with a stole over her head and shoulders, and her English was impeccable. She came from an aristocratic family who owned large swathes of land in Sindh, in southern Pakistan, and went on to become a global icon.

After her father, a former prime minister, was hanged following General Zia's coup d'état, she succeeded him at the head of the Pakistan People's Party—the PPP—which she would rule with a rod of iron until her death. On the numerous occasions she was forced into exile, she continued to direct it from abroad.

On August 17, 1988, Zia was killed when his airplane crashed, and on December 2, Benazir Bhutto became prime minister— the first female elected head of a Muslim country. Her first term lasted only twenty months, as she was dismissed by President Ghulam Ishaq Khan for corruption and abuse of power. She was replaced by Nawaz Sharif, who, in turn, was accused of corruption in 1993. Benazir was restored to her post on the basis of a fragile coalition.

Having learned from her mistakes, this time she formed an alliance with the army and raised her profile on the international stage. However, things started to go awry following the assassination of her increasingly popular brother, Murtaza, which some accused her of orchestrating. Again, there was talk of corruption, especially with regard to her husband, Zardari, known as "Mr. 10 Percent" after the commission he charged in exchange for government contracts. Her second term of office ended in 1996, when the president dismissed her government on the grounds of incompetence and corruption. The military had begun to put obstacles in her way, and the couple was accused by the Swiss justice system of money laundering.

Exiled to Dubai, she worked on her image in order to appear moderate and indispensable at the head of the country that was the only nuclear power in the Islamic world. In 2007, Benazir and her husband were granted an amnesty by Musharraf. Back in Karachi, on October 18 she escaped a suicide bombing that killed two hundred people, but two months later she was not so lucky. On December 27, 2007, she was assassinated in Rawalpindi.

Benazir Bhutto in Pakistan,
November 14, 1988.

AUNG SAN SUU KYI

(born 1945)

She was once seen as an icon in the West: some compared her to Nelson Mandela, others to Gandhi or Martin Luther King, Jr. Striking and courageous, the Lady of Rangoon was the staunch defender of the rights of the Burmese people against a merciless military junta.

Daughter of an independence leader assassinated when she was two years old, Aung San Suu Kyi went to live with her mother, ambassador in New Delhi, where she studied at the University of Delhi, before proceeding to Oxford University. There she met Michael Aris, a Briton whom she married, remaining by his side in the 1970s and 1980s.

In 1988, she returned to Burma to visit her ailing mother and was struck by the violence of military rule: surrounded by soldiers, hundreds of students were beaten to death. She entered politics as the daughter of Aung San, a hero admired by Burmese youth, and founded the National League for Democracy (NLD). This led to her arrest and, refusing to leave the country as requested, she was placed under house arrest, which was to last fifteen years. Despite this, in the 1990 elections the NLD won by a wide margin. However, the results were annulled by the military, causing international outcry.

The same year, she won both the Nobel Peace Prize and the Sakharov Prize, but was prevented from receiving either personally; nor was she permitted to leave the country to visit her husband who was terminally ill with cancer. Some say that she sacrificed her personal life to politics.

The clouds began to lift in 2010, when she was finally released from house arrest. In 2012, she was elected member of Parliament and was at last given leave to receive her Nobel Prize in Oslo. Her party won the elections in 2015, but soon the Lady of Rangoon was seen to have feet of clay. Just like Indira Gandhi (see p. 140), Benazir Bhutto (see p. 144), and Chandrika Kumaratunga, she had come to power thanks to the name of her martyred father but gradually became authoritarian, despotic even. She was soon unrecognizable.

Unmoved by the ongoing genocide of the Muslim Rohingya, she denied the reality of the ethnic cleansing. Long idolized, her halo has well and truly slipped.

Aung San Suu Kyi in Singapore, November 30, 2016.

CORAZON AQUINO

(1933–2009)

Following light-fingered embezzler Ferdinand Marcos and his wife Imelda—"the Iron Butterfly," known for her three thousand pairs of shoes—came Corazon Aquino, nicknamed the upright and very Catholic "St. Cory."

This self-effacing young woman from a family of major landowners married Benigno (Ninoy) Aquino, who was a journalist, then mayor, governor, and senator. She handed round the canapés and took care of her five children—until 1983, when Ninoy was murdered by Marcos's henchmen. The opposition then turned to her, urging her to enter politics. After some hesitation, she ran in the 1985 elections, a poll so rigged that a million demonstrators poured into the streets of Manila. The United States ushered Marcos into exile, and Corazon Aquino became the Philippines' seventh president and its first woman head of state.

Possessed of exemplary moral credentials, including unimpeachable honesty—the same could not be said of her coterie, especially her brother—Cory was inexperienced and indecisive. However, she succeeded in releasing many political prisoners, and pushed through a new constitution. Breaking the monopoly on sugar cane and coconut, she reduced taxes on fuel, seeds, and fertilizer, which gained her immense popularity. On the foreign affairs front, the United States and Japan injected billions of dollars to drag the archipelago out of recession. The problem was that the money bypassed the poor and went to the wealthy minorities. Gradually the gap between rich and poor widened.

Political life in the Philippines has long been marked by putsches. Cory was on the receiving end of seven, all quashed thanks to army chief General Ramos and, in 1989, American intervention. But by that time, her only support came from the Catholic Church. Eschewing reelection in 1992, she stood aside for Ramos in a peaceful handover that was unusual in her homeland. Her presidency marked the return of democracy and freedom.

Philippine president Corazon Aquino hails the crowd at a victory rally in Manila on March 2, 1986, following the People Power Revolution.

NEW ZEALAND'S WOMEN LEADERS

This unique and beautiful country has long been a paradise for women's rights and equality.

New Zealand—*Aotearoa* for the Maori—gave women the right to vote in 1893, well before the rest of the world, especially thanks to suffragist Kate Sheppard, whose face now appears on the NZ$10 bill. In 2013, *The Economist* ranked it as the most egalitarian country for women, ahead even of Norway and Sweden.

Women have held all the major political posts: queen, with Elizabeth II and Te Atairangikaahu, Queen of the Maori; Governor General, with Patsy Reddy (since 2016); prime minister, with Jenny Shipley (1997), Helen Clark (1999), and now Jacinda Ardern; not forgetting Speaker of the House of Representatives (Margaret Wilson) and Chief Justice (Sian Elias).

The most famous are undoubtedly the prime ministers. Labour politician and anti-militarist Helen Clark was reelected twice, serving three terms. Active against the Vietnam War, she opposed the conflict in Iraq. A committed environmentalist, she was the first female administrator of the UN Development Programme.

The other prime minister whose picture is ubiquitous today is Jacinda Ardern. Joining the Labour Party at the age of seventeen, she worked with then party leader Helen Clark, before moving to New York and London where she became political adviser to Tony Blair. Returning to New Zealand in 2008, she became the youngest member of Parliament and then youngest Labour Party leader in the country's history. Coalition prime minister since 2017, the thirty-eight-year-old is charismatic, compassionate, and generous. Her pregnancy surprised outsiders—the only other head of government to have been pregnant while in office was Benazir Bhutto (see p. 144)—as did her six-week maternity leave. She took her young daughter, sporting a "New Zealand First Baby" badge, to the UN General Assembly. Her dignity after the terrorist massacre in Christchurch further bolstered her popularity and sparked "Jacindamania."

Clockwise, from top left:
Portrait of suffragist Kate Sheppard
by Henry Herbert Clifford, c. 1905.
Maori queen Te Arikinui Dame
Te Atairangikaahu, March 16, 1999.
Jacinda Ardern in 2020.
Helen Clark in 2009.

Pages 152–53:
During a demonstration in 1935
in favor of women's suffrage,
at Place de la Bastille in Paris,
members of the movement
La Femme Nouvelle,
launched by Louise Weiss,
throw chains onto a bonfire.

Bibliography

GENERAL READING

ASHBY, Ruth, and Deborah GORE OHRN, eds. *Herstory: Women Who Changed the World.* Preface by Gloria Steinem. New York: Viking, 1995.

BELGIQUE, Esmeralda de. *Femmes prix Nobel de la paix.* Brussels: Avant-Propos, 2014.

GAUTHIER, Xavière. *Women of Consequence: Heroines Who Shaped the World.* Paris: Flammarion, 2010.

AFRICA AND THE MIDDLE EAST

"The Thirty Tyrants." In *Historia Augusta.* Translated by David Magie. Cambridge, MA: Loeb Classical Library, Harvard University Press, 1924.

ALFRED, Cyril, Paul BARQUET, Christiane DESROCHES NOBLECOURT, Hans WOLFGANG-MÜLLER, and Jean LECLANT. *L'Empire des conquérants: L'Égypte au Nouvel Empire (1560–1070 avant J.-C.).* Paris: Gallimard, 1979.

CAMPS, Gabriel. *L'Afrique du Nord au féminin.* Paris: Perrin, 1992.

CAVAZZI, Giovanni-Antonio. *Njinga, reine d'Angola.* Paris: Chandeigne, 2014.

DESROCHES NOBLECOURT, Christiane. *La Reine mystérieuse: Hatshepsout.* Paris: Pygmalion, 2002.

HEYWOOD, Linda M. *Njinga of Angola: Africa's Warrior Queen.* Cambridge, MA: Harvard University Press, 2019.

IBN KHALDÛN. *The Muqaddimah: An Introduction to History.* Translated and introduced by Franz Rosenthal. Abridged and edited by N. J. Dawood. With an introduction by Bruce B. Lawerence. New York: Princeton University Press, 2015.

KIEJMAN, Claude-Catherine. *Golda Meir: Une vie pour Israël.* Paris: Tallandier, 2016.

LALOUETTE, Claire. *Histoire de la civilisation pharaonique II. Thèbes ou la naissance d'un empire.* Paris: Flammarion, 1995.

SACKHO-AUTISSIER, Aminata. "Les Candaces, des reines régnantes." In *Méroé, un empire sur le Nil.* Edited by Michel Baud. Paris: Musée du Louvre, 2010.

SARTRE, Maurice, and Annie SARTRE-FAURIAT. *Palmyre, la cité des caravanes.* Paris: Gallimard, 2008.

THESIGER, Wilfred. *The Life of My Choice.* London: Harper Collins, 1987.

EUROPE AND RUSSIA

ATKINSON, Diane. *The Remarkable Lives of the Suffragettes.* London: Bloomsbury Publishing, 2018.

AUTRET, Florence. *Angela Merkel : Une Allemande (presque) comme les autres.* Paris: Tallandier, 2013.

BADINTER, Élisabeth. *Le Pouvoir au féminin: Marie-Thérèse d'Autriche (1717-1780), l'impératrice reine.* Paris: Flammarion, 2016.

BEAUNE, Colette. *Jeanne d'Arc.* Paris: Perrin, 2009.

BLED, Jean-Paul. *Marie-Thérèse d'Autriche.* Paris: Fayard, 2001.

CARACCIOLO, Maria Teresa. *Les Sœurs de Napoléon: Trois destins italiens.* Paris: Hazan, 2013.

CARATINI, Roger. *Jeanne d'Arc: De Domrémy à Orléans et du bûcher à la légende.* Paris: L'Archipel, 2011.

CATHERINE II. *Memoirs of the Empress Catherine II of Russia.* Preface by Alexander Herzen. London: Trübner and Co., 1859.

COLLINGRIDGE, Vanessa. *Boudica.* London: Ebury Press, 2006.

DESPRAT, Jean-Paul. *Madame de Maintenon (1635-1719) ou le prix de la réputation.* Paris: Perrin, 2010.

DOWNEY, Kirstin. *Isabella, the Warrior Queen.* New York: Nan A. Talese/ Doubleday, 2014.

DUBOST, Jean-François. *Marie de Médicis: La Reine dévoilée.* Paris: Payot, 2009.

DUBY, Georges. *Dames du XIIe siècle : Héloïse, Aliénor, Iseut et quelques autres.* Paris: Gallimard, 1995.

FLORI, Jean. *Aliénor d'Aquitaine: La Reine insoumise.* Paris: Payot, 2004.

GIROD, Virginie. *Les Femmes et le sexe dans la Rome antique.* Paris: Tallandier, 2017.

GRIMAL, Pierre. *L'Amour à Rome.* Paris: Les Belles Lettres, 1988.

GRUEL-APERT, Lise. *De la paysanne à la tsarine: La Russie traditionnelle côté femmes.* Paris: Imago, 2007.

HARGROVE, Charles. *La Reine.* Paris: Librairie académique Perrin, 1994.

HENNESSY, Peter. *The Prime Minister: The Office and Its Holders Since 1945.* London: Allen Lane, 2000.

HEYDEN-RYNSCH, Verena von der. *Christine de Suède: La souveraine énigmatique.* Paris: Gallimard, 2001.

HIBBERT, Christopher. *Queen Victoria: A Personal History.* London: Harper Collins, 2000.

———. *The Virgin Queen: A Personal History of Elizabeth I.* London: Tauris Parke Paperbacks, 2010.

LA CROIX DE CASTRIES, René de. *La Pompadour.* Paris: Albin Michel, 1983.

LANGLADE, Jacques de. *La Reine Victoria.* Paris: Perrin, 2000.

LEVER, Evelyne. *Madame de Pompadour.* Paris: Perrin, 2000.

LIECHTENHAN, Francine-Dominique. *Élisabeth Ire de Russie, l'autre impératrice.* Paris: Fayard, 2007.

LIGNE, Charles-Joseph de. *Lettres et pensées du Prince de Ligne.* Introduced and annotated by Raymond Trousson. Paris: Tallandier, 1989.

MARR, Andrew. *The Diamond Queen: Elizabeth II and Her People.* London: Pan Books, 2012.

MASSIE, Robert K. *Catherine the Great: Portrait of a Woman.* New York: Random House, 2011.

ORLÉANS, Anne-Marie-Louise de. *Mémoires de la Grande Mademoiselle.* London: Modern Humanities Research Association, 2010.

PERROT, Michelle. *Des femmes rebelles.* Paris: Elyzad, 2014.

PROCOPIUS. *The Secret History.* Edited, translated, and with an introduction by Peter Sarris. Translated by G. A. Williamson. London: Penguin Classics, 2007.

SAINT-SIMON, Louis de. *Historical Memoirs of the Duc de Saint-Simon.* Vols. I–III. Edited and translated by Lucy Norton. London: Hamish Hamilton, 1967, 1968, 1972.

SCHMIDT, Joël. *Louise de Prusse: La reine qui défia Napoléon.* Paris: Perrin, 1995.

SÉVIGNÉ, Marie de. *Madame de Sévigné: Selected Letters.* Translated and introduced by Leonard Tancock. London: Penguin Classics, 1982.

SOLNON, Jean-François. *Catherine de Médicis.* Paris: Perrin, 2003.

STRACHEY, Lytton. *Queen Victoria.* San Diego, CA: Harcourt Brace Jovanovich, [1921], 2002.

SUETONIUS. *The Life of the Twelve Caesars.* Translated by Robert Graves. Revised with an introduction and notes by J. B. Rive. London: Penguin Classics, [1957], rev. ed. 2007.

TACITUS. *The Agricola and the Germania.* Edited by S. A. Handford. Translated by H. Mattingly. London: Penguin Classics, [1948], rev. ed. 1971.

TURNER, Ralph V. *Eleanor of Aquitaine.* New Haven, CT: Yale University Press, 2011.

VEIL, Simone. *A Life.* Translated by Tamsin Black. London: Haus Publishing, 2009.

VIDAL, Florence. *Élisa Bonaparte.* Paris: Flammarion, 2005.

WEISS, Louise. *Mémoires d'une Européenne.* Paris: Payot, 1968.

THE AMERICAS

FRASER, Nicholas, and Marysa NAVARRO. *Evita: The Real Life of Eva Perón.* New York: Norton, 1980.

LAGOMARSINO DE GUARDO, Lillian. *Y ahora… hablo yo.* Buenos Aires: Editorial Sudamericana, 1996.

OCKRENT, Christine. *La Double vie d'Hillary Clinton.* Paris: Robert Laffont, 2001.

ROBIEN, Beata de. *Les Passions d'une présidente: Eleanor Roosevelt.* Paris: Perrin, 2000.

ASIA PACIFIC

CASTRO, Mercedes. *Indira Gandhi: La Femme d'État qui bouleversa l'histoire de l'Inde.* Barcelona: RBA, 2020.

CLÉMENT, Catherine. *La Reine des Cipayes.* Paris: Le Seuil, 2012.

DEVI, Gayatri. *A Princess Remembers: Memoirs of the Maharani of Jaipur.* New Delhi: Rupa Publications, 1995.

ELISSEEFF, Danielle. *La Femme au temps des empereurs de Chine.* Paris: Stock, 1988.

———. *Cixi, impératrice de Chine.* Paris: Perrin, 2008.

GANDHI, Indira. *My Truth.* New York: Grove Atlantic, 1982.

JIN Yi. *Mémoires d'une dame de cour dans la Cité interdite.* Arles: Picquier, 1993.

LAFRANCE, Pierre. *Du temps de Benazir Bhutto.* Paris: Gnôsis Éditions de France, 2008.

LANG, John. *Wanderings in India, and Other Sketches of Life in Hindostan.* London: Routledge, Warne, and Routledge, 1859.

LA RONCIÈRE, Bertrand de. *La Reine Pomaré : Tahiti et l'Occident, 1812-1877.* Paris: L'Harmattan, 2003.

PATE, Alan-Scott. *Ningyo: The Art of the Japanese Doll.* Boston: Tuttle, 2005.

PHILIP, Bruno. *Aung San Suu Kyi : L'Icône fracassée.* Paris: Équateurs, 2017.

RICAUD, Louis, and Toan NGHIEM. *Wou Tsö – Tien.* Linear translation and commentary of the official biography of the empress. Paris: Bulletin de la Société des Études indochinoises, 1959.

How can I thank you?

Should we start with those
who helped the most? "First and
foremost, I would like to thank
my husband, François Gaulme."
Or do we save them for the end,
as a grand finale? "And finally,
none of this would have been
possible without my husband,
François Gaulme." In short,
without him, neither you nor I
would have had the good fortune
of encountering Louise of Prussia,
Napoleon's most ravishing
adversary. Nor Matilda of Tuscany,
who flashed up on my computer
screen, along with an indignant
"Haven't you put Matilda in?"
Or "And Canossa? Doesn't Canossa
ring any bells with you?"
So, a huge thank-you to him.

Next, I wish to thank my American
friends: Eleanor Heginbotham,
an Emily Dickinson specialist
who is practically my sister;
Nicole Hopson, another "almost
sister" from New York; and
Clémentine Letouzé, yet another
"almost sister" and New Yorker
turned Parisian. They helped me
to make my selection from among
the many great women of
the Americas.

I owe the suggestion of Kahina,
queen of Awras, to my dear friend
Kathy Wendling. She also provided
material on the mysterious Jingu
of Japan.

Thank you to Olivier Bouzy,
a medieval historian and
Joan of Arc specialist, whom I saw
in Orléans, and to Philippe Sellier,
who is always keen to make it
known that the "Précieuses" were
not at all "*ridicules*."

And where would researchers be
without great libraries and great
librarians? Thank you to those
who helped me at the Paris
City Hall library, the Académie
des Sciences d'Outre-Mer, the
École Française d'Extrême-Orient,
and the Bibliothèque Marguerite
Durand.

157

Design and Typesetting
  Marie Pellaton

Cover Design
  Audrey Sednaoui

Picture Research
  Marie-Catherine Audet
  and Aude Laporte

French Edition

Editorial Director
  Julie Rouart

Administration Manager
  Delphine Montagne

Senior Editor
  Gaëlle Lassée
  assisted by Clarisse Moreno

English Edition

Editorial Director
  Kate Mascaro

Editor
  Helen Adedotun

Foreword by
  Lindsay Porter

Translated from the French by
  David Radzinowicz

Copyediting
  Lindsay Porter

Proofreading
  Sarah Kane

Production
  Margot Jourdan

Color Separation
  Reproscan, Bergamo, Italy

Printed in Portugal by
  Printer Portuguesa

This work is based on an original idea
by Elisabeth Sandmann Verlag GmbH,
Munich.

Simultaneously published in French as
Les Femmes de pouvoir sont dangereuses
© Flammarion, S.A., Paris, 2020

English-language edition
© Flammarion, S.A., Paris, 2020

20 21 22   3 2 1

ISBN: 978-2-08-020672-5

Legal Deposit: 11/2020